Echoes fr

To Sherry
I love your
stories poems and
especially the art work
Thank you
Ruth Butler

By Ruth Butler

*To my son Bruce and my granddaughter Jennifer
for encouraging me to share my stories*

Chapter 1

I could see the coyote up on the hill. He was always there. He always watched me. I often glanced toward him to be sure he didn't start down across the field. I wondered why he always sat in the same place to watch. I tried not to let him see me looking at him for fear it would make him mad.

I sat in a furrow waiting for Papa to make it around the big field with the plow. The rich black earth beside me had sheen on the smooth side where the shiny plow shear had sliced into it and turned it over. In the far distance, I saw Papa approaching. Not long ago I'd heard him complaining to Mama about the steel seat with holes in it he had to sit on. I worried about him having to sit on the seat all day.

"It makes me sore as the devil. Don't know why they put them holes in that darn hard steel seat. My backside squeezes out through those little holes and shuts off the circulation until it feels like it's paralyzed after sitting on it all day."

I didn't know what paralyzed meant but it sounded like something awful bad.

I knew Mama had put on her thinking cap when she came up with her answer, "I could make you a leather cushion out of some of that leather hanging in the well house and stuff it with goose down and chicken feathers."

Goody, I thought, that will get even with that old goose for chasing me and snapping at my legs. But Papa thought otherwise.

"No Anna, I'm figuring on selling that leather we made from all those hides when we butchered. I can get a good price and besides you got enough to do already. We need all your feathers to finish filling that feather-tic so we can replace the ones on the bunkhouse beds. Feathers are a lot nicer to sleep on than the straw filled tics we have in there now. Maybe we can make you something nice out of the ermine or beaver we trapped. How about making a fur collar to put on your coat?"

"Oh Claude, that would be so nice you know I've always wanted one. They are so popular now."

I liked sitting on the damp ground thinking about things while I was waiting for Papa. The sun felt so warm on my back. A few weeks before there were patches of snow and I jumped across little rivers the melting snow made. Now I could smell the earth warming. Everything around me spoke of spring. I heard a meadowlark. I breathed spring in the air and I could see tinges of green in the big field on the far hill that would soon be a green carpet of growing grain. A strong feeling of contentment closed around me like the feeling of being held in Mama's arms.

Papa always plowed some fields in the fall after he harvested the grain. Papa called it summer fallow. Then he planted the grain and the snow covered the ground all winter. During the spring thaw the snow melted and the ground warmed up. Then all the hills as far as the eye could see turned a lush green until later when summer breathed her warm breath across the land and turned the wheat fields to gold.

Today Papa had plowed the field close to the house where he wanted to plant seed potatoes. He put a saddle blanket on old Dan and let me ride one lap around with him. It was a long ways and I thought I might be getting paralyzed so I only wanted to go once.

While I waited for him, I took my shoes off and set them on a clod of dirt. I usually went barefoot anyway. I wiggled my toes and fingers in the soft, crumbly earth. It felt good.

All of a sudden, my toe scratched against something. I dug around with my fingers to see what it was. I pulled and tugged at the strange object. Finally, it came loose and I brushed some dirt away. I found a small rock and started scratching and digging the rest of the dirt from it. It was then it became a shape. What a wonderful treasure I had found! A toy train locomotive made of iron. It was rusty and old but it couldn't have made me happier if it had been Christmas morning.

This beautiful experience of one day in spring became one of my earliest childhood memories that I tucked away forever in my patchwork of memories.

When I looked up, Papa and the big horses Dick and Dan were coming toward me. I picked up my buried treasure and ran to show

Papa.

"Papa, Papa, look what I found!"

He pulled back on the reins attached to the bit in the mouth of the horses.

"Whoa there Dick, Dan!"

Dick and Dan were ready to whoa after a long hard day. Their backs dripped sweat and they switched their tails and tossed their heads up and down to shoo away the pesky horse flies swarming around them.

"Let's see what you found Ruthie. Well, I'll be darned. How do you suppose that toy ever got out here in the field? I guess some little girl like you must have been playing with it here."

Papa seemed as excited as I was. He turned the train over again looking at it.

"Might be a rare find. Come here and I'll sit you on Dan's back and you can ride him to the barn, then you can give Dick and Dan their oats."

Papa unhooked Dick and Dan from the plow and walked behind them with the reins still in his hands. It hurt to sit on the harness but I didn't tell Papa. Inside the barn, he lifted the heavy harness off the horses' backs and hung it on hooks on the wall behind the stalls. I heard the bells on the harness tinkle softly. Dick and Dan got their oats special from me and Papa patted them on the back as if to say thanks.

In those days, the snow got so high in the winter that we couldn't travel by car and we went most places in a covered sleigh behind Dick and Dan. They were Papa's two favorite horses. He had several other horses because all the farming equipment was horse drawn and it took several horses to pull the combine when he harvested the grain.

What a pretty sight it was to watch all those horses run across the pasture kicking up their heels and tossing their heads with nostrils flaring when they saw Papa bringing them a couple of buckets of oats for the evening treat. How lucky can a little girl be to get to live on a farm? I loved horses and I wished Mama wouldn't worry so much about me getting around them.

"How many times do I have to tell you to stay out of the corral? Some of these days one of those horses is going to kick your head off when you get too close to him. Remember when one kicked the neighbor? They run wild most of the time and they aren't like the saddle ponies. Now come back in the yard and play with your stick horses."

It was late and the sun would soon be gone. There were still other chores to do. Papa hurried. The tantalizing smell of Mama's fried chicken floated through the air from the house.

Papa sniffed the air and hurried even faster.

"I'm hungry as a horse Ruthie. How about you? What all did you do today besides sit on the damp ground? Your sister will have a fit when she sees your dirty clothes and dirty feet and all that dirt under your fingernails."

My big sister Mabel didn't like me to get even a little bit dirty. It seems her mission in life was to keep me clean and neat and she would rather have me in dresses than coveralls but Mama thought dresses weren't very practical there on the farm.

Papa finished the chores and fed the stock. He split some wood for Mama to cook tomorrow's meals on our new kitchen range. I looked to see if the coyote was still there on the hill. He was.

Mama was standing by the range stirring gravy when we finally went in the house. We hurried to wash up at the washbasin sitting on the washstand so we could eat with the two hired men already sitting at the table drinking coffee and chatting.

"How did the disking on the far field go today?" Papa asked the men.

"We just about finished up. Guess we can start harrowing tomorrow if we get the harrow fixed."

Mama looked fondly at the stove as she poured the gravy in a bowl and put it in the warming oven to keep it warm until she mashed the potatoes. She took several ears of corn out of a big kettle she used for canning and stacked them on a platter.

"Could you run and get a dish full of butter out of the butter crock in the ice box Ruthie? That's a good girl. Thank you very much."

I could tell how much Mama loved that monster cook stove but no wonder she liked it so much. The big stove had a reservoir on the side to store hot water. The water in the reservoir was heated by coils in the firebox. Before she got her new kitchen stove she had to heat water in two teakettles on top of the old stove. The new oven was twice as big so she could bake larger amounts of bread. The stove had fancy decorations that shined brightly and the gray speckled color of the stove added to the luster and grandeur that fit the name Monarch Kitchen Range.

I remember the day the peddler came to sell us the new kitchen stove.

He had a little replica of what our stove would look like when it came. You can never imagine how cute that little stove was and how much I wanted it. It was just my size.

"Does Santa have a stove like that?"

"No little girl, I'm sure he doesn't have a little stove like this one. The Monarch Range Company had these special made to show our customers."

I thought he could tell how much I wanted that little stove so I followed him out to his peddler type wagon and watched him juggling pots and pans hanging on the outside. There was lots of other stuff too. He probably thought he might as well try to pawn some of that off while he was here.

I put on my best sad face as I watched thinking he might feel sorry for me and give me the little stove. He took one look at my best sad face then suddenly he crawled up in the seat and said, "Giddy up" to his old plug of a horse and drove off leaving me standing there in the middle of the road without so as much as a goodbye.

Chapter 2

Not too long after I found the toy train, I got to ride on a real train. It was only a short way from Drummond, Idaho to Lamont, Idaho to visit Aunt Ed.

"All aboard! All aboard! Everyone aboard that's coming aboard. Lamont, Driggs, Victor," shouted a man in a blue uniform while he swung a lantern back and forth.

I don't know why he had a lantern. It was broad daylight. Papa said he was the conductor. I didn't know what conductor meant but he acted like he was the boss.

Not many people climbed up the metal steps to board the train, just Mama and Papa, my sister Mabel, my brother Rex and me.

"Hello, little girl. You going for a ride on the train? What's your name? Can you tell me how old you are? What's the matter cat got your tongue?"

I hid behind Mama.

We found our seats and they let me sit by the window. Then the man with the lantern came and stood in the aisle beside us only he didn't have the lantern. He had a puncher in his hand now.

"May I see your tickets please?"

He punched each ticket with the ticket puncher and then stuck them over our seats in a ticket holder.

Who would ever dream there was anything so different from our Model T. Ford to ride in? I sat on red velvet-like plush seats and smelled the strange smells that are hard to describe and I heard the puzzling noises. The engine huffed and puffed and something else made clinking and clanging noises. The wheels went clink click on the rails. Through the window, speckled with dirty snow spots, I could see the steam pouring from the train's smoke stack floating around in the cold air. It rolled to the ground and then wrapped around the wheels.

I saw a man Papa called the stoker stoking the burner to make the steam that ran the steam engine in the locomotive. Then he sat down by a man with a striped cap that drove the train. Papa said he was the engineer.

There was a snowplow on the front of the cowcatcher and the snow flew over to the side away from the train tracks. Papa explained everything to me. That's how I know all this about everything.

I never rode on that train again but I have always carried the memory of my great adventure with me and often play this mental tape over again on my mind in my old age. I watch a little girl's big adventure on a train once again and feel the same excitement of an important day of her life and that little girl is me.

Chapter 3

The winters in that part of Idaho close to the Rocky Mountains where I lived as a child were very severe but I think the weather is much milder there now. Our summers were another extreme and got what Papa called blazing hot. The wind blew all the time, summer and winter. A hot, dry wind dried everything out in the summer. During the winter, cold winds brought blustering blizzards. The weather caused all kinds of hardships for my family. The day of my birth was one of the hardships made even harder because of the weather.

My parents had recently moved from Oregon to Idaho to live on a farm near Drummond. The road past our farm was not open in winter and we could only travel by horses pulling a sleigh. Because of the roads, my folks had moved from the farm into Drummond, a small nearby town, to spend the winter months. I was born in the house at Drummond on Thanksgiving Day, November 30, 1922 during one of those terrible blustery blizzards.

The only doctor in the area had his practice in Ashton, another small town a few miles from Drummond. Because the roads out of Ashton were impassable that day in the blizzard, the doctor came by train to help Mama deliver her little bundle of joy. Me. He stayed with us all night and returned to Ashton next day on the train. My birth and the blizzard ruined his Thanksgiving and I kind of wonder if Mama would have rather had a turkey for Thanksgiving than me.

There is no record of my birth in the Idaho Bureau of Vital

Statistics. I guess rural areas often neglected to record births when children were born at home. Unlike earlier times when the doctors made house-calls most women were going to hospitals to give birth. It was unusual not to be born in a hospital during the time I was born when America was first emerging into our new modern world. The area where we lived was too far from a hospital and local doctors still made house calls.

My family continued to live the hard life of previous generations with no modern advantages. It seems to me now that it was almost like they had been caught up in a time warp and stuck there beyond the hills in Idaho. I'm thankful they made the choice to live like they did for it gave me some of my greatest memories. It was an impressive time in my life and I have never forgotten the things I learned and the joy of that wonderful time I had living on a farm with my family when I was a child. My memories have become my most valuable possessions.

Nowadays, instead of living in a time warp of the past, I feel as though I am caught up in a fast forward mode of life. Everything and every day and everybody speeds past me at a much faster pace until days months and years are so brief I can hardly believe where the time has gone. Everyone is in such a hurry rushing from one commitment to another there is never time to notice people. We often don't visit our next-door neighbors or even know them or what is going on around us. Hurry, Hurry, Hurry.

My early childhood was much different on the farm than that of the children living in town. In fact, my whole life has been very unusual and filled with change every few years. Sometimes I hear stories from the lives of other people who had wealth and knowledge or what we consider the good life but I never feel envy. I wouldn't change anything, although extreme sorrow and hard times have filled my life many times. It taught me to appreciate the good times and how lucky I've been to have the people I loved and who loved me.

At the time of my birth, Thanksgiving was always the last Thursday of November. My birthday only fell on Thanksgiving one time after being born on such an important holiday. This happened because leap year changed the days every four years and moved Thanksgiving.

Now I wonder. Does this make me a lot younger than I am because I didn't have as many birthdays on the day I should have? It seems like I've heard something like that about regular leap year babies.

To add to the confusion President Roosevelt changed Thanksgiving to an earlier date instead of the last Thursday of November to make Christmas shopping season last longer. He did this to stimulate the economy during the Great Depression.

People used to put their Christmas shopping off until after Thanksgiving. But after Thanksgiving Day was changed shopping day changed too and started after Labor Day. That's when we first saw early Christmas decorations and gifts start appearing in the stores.

I'm not sure but I believe that has changed again and Christmas shopping for next Christmas starts the day after New Year's Day. Anyway, there seems to be a lot of people shopping for left over Christmas items after Christmas. Not me, I like the last minute rush shoving and pushing for gifts. It makes it seem like Christmas to save Christmas until it is really here.

When I was very young there were only two days of Christmas. We decorated the tree Papa cut, strung garlands of popcorn and cranberries, made green and red popcorn balls and went to church to see Santa for the first time that year. There was only one Santa and he never showed up around Drummond until Christmas.

It's funny how memories pop in unexpectedly and interrupt my story. Now while I'm writing about the day I was born, which I don't remember at all, I recall something from when I was about three.

"Mama, where did I come from?" I wonder why most children ask this same question.

I know now that I've had children of my own the question startled her and she didn't know how she should answer.

"My darling baby we found you in a snow bank."

It must have sounded very believable because I started looking for babies everywhere. I hoped for a baby sister to play with.

Of course, I never found a baby but one time Mama's belly got so big she wouldn't let me climb in her lap and told me to stay down. This denial hurt my feelings and I pouted my lips at her for days when she wouldn't let me take my place on her lap.

Then one day not too long after that I heard Mama yelling and screaming in the bedroom. Doctor Meacham came rushing into the house carrying a black bag and he went into the bedroom with Mama. I did not know what to do because I was so scared and worried. Some woman told me to go outside and play.

"Your Mama is very sick, but don't worry. Doctor will make her well. Now go on outside Ruthie."

I went outside and sat on the step with Papa and I started crying. He cried too and it made me cry even more. I had never seen Papa cry.

I never knew what happened that day until I was grown and Mama told me I had a little sister but she died at birth. They buried her down by the old house. The empty old house on our property still holds many happy memories of those years in my life so I'm glad Mama never told me about my baby sister's grave when I was little.

The impressions my birthplace made on my life are some of the most valuable things I could have inherited from that time of my life. My love for the outdoor life I lived then gave me many moments of peace and tranquility all through my life as I followed my wanderlust always wondering about other places in our great outdoors all across America. I've seen so many places, done so many unusual things, and met so many people I could never crowd it all in one book.

My favorite towns have always been the little towns that remind me of Ashton and Drummond. People greet everyone, even strangers, with a smile and a hello. I've noticed in some crowded busy cities they have frowny faces and seem not to even notice there are other people around. I seldom see a smiley face or hear a friendly hello and when I offer these friendly gestures to people they stare at me like I am a strange bulldog or I'm weird.

A few years ago, a woman smiled at me as I waited inside the door of a building for the door to open so I could ride my mobility scooter out. It was such a pleasant smile and it made my day. I felt the sincerity behind her smile. It inspired me to write a poem.

WHEN YOU SMILE
There was a twinkle in your eye when you smiled at me today.
You made my day complete in your own special way.
You made me happy.

I didn't know who you were and I didn't know your name.
You didn't know me either but you smiled just the same.
It was a friendly smile.
Your smile lingered with me as I went down the street.
And I wondered. Do you smile at everyone you meet?
Or was I special?
It made me feel so happy when you gave me your smile.
If I never see you again at least I met you for a while.
Have a nice day.

I often give a copy of my poem to people I meet when they give me a special smile.

Chapter 4

Weather played a large part in the way we lived during my early childhood. Papa dry farmed a thousand acres of hilly land west of the Grand Teton Range of the Rocky Mountains in Idaho not far from Yellowstone Park. Our place was just across the mountain from Jackson Hole, Wyoming. We lived between two of the most interesting and beautiful places I've ever seen in all my travels.

Since there is no irrigation on a dry farm the crops depend on rain during the summer but often there isn't enough rain and sometimes there's too much.

I remember a few hailstorms with hailstones as big as golf balls (not an exaggeration). They beat the wheat to the ground and pounded the horses and cow so hard they fell to their knees. We watched the hailstorms from the front porch as they destroyed crops and punished animals.

"Why are you putting on your mackinaw coat Claude? You aren't thinking of going out in this hail storm are you?"

"I have to go put the animals in the barn. You see what the hail is doing? We can't afford to lose some of them too. The crop is already gone."

"I don't care! I'm worried about Rex out in this some place. I don't want to worry about you too."

As I recall this memory of that day, I see in my mind a picture of Papa standing with his hands made into fists as he watches the wheat fall flat in the fields and his animals suffer from the beating of the hail. He is helpless to do anything to stop it.

I feel the silence after the noise of the hail stopped and hear Mama sobbing. There is hail piled all over the ground. The sun is shining brightly and the hailstones glisten. The storm crept in like the thief it was and raged for a short while then rolled away across the hills leaving behind a scene of destruction. I could still hear echoes of thunder rumbling from the distant hills.

I glanced up on the hill wondering if the coyote had made it through the storm. He was still standing there in the same place.

"Where is Rex in all this?"

Mama panicked because my brother had ridden his horse to town and didn't return until hours later. When he finally came riding in Mama grabbed him and hugged him.

"I was worried to death about you. Where were you? Did you get hailed on? It was terrible here. I was just going to send Papa to look for you when I saw you coming around the corner by the old house. Thank God you are alright."

"Oh Mama, you worry too much. I was in Thorten's house all the time and it wasn't as bad there as it looks here."

It made me feel happy to watch Mama because she was so relieved. I hugged Rex too.

I shudder now even thinking about the frightening electric storms we often had that cracked and sent jagged streaks of lightning across the sky to the ground. The claps of thunder were so loud with sharp cracking sounds they seemed to be right in the room with us.

I've never been any place where thunder echoed through the hills like it did Idaho. The sound seemed to roll as it bounced over rocky hills and through valleys and canyons. You could hear it as it moved away like a speeding car with those roaring exhaust pipes I hear late at night that young people seem to enjoy so much these days.

Mama was so afraid of the electric storms. She took me to bed and we covered our heads with blankets so we couldn't see or hear it. I'm still afraid of lightning and thunder.

Another weather event that is stored in my memory bank was a cyclone that circled across one of Papa's fields. We watched as it lifted everything it touched and swirled it around in the sky. Boards and scraps of buildings and dust clumps of wheat all went twirling around. It shattered a storage building in the wheat field to pieces and carried it away. It frightened Mama and me but we didn't hide in bed this time. We huddled together and watched from the porch.

I've always wondered about the following story Papa told us:

"I once heard a man say he saw a cyclone drive a straw through a fence post and lift a house up and move it over a hundred feet."

Mama spoofed at that story.

"You don't believe that do you Claude? I think I know who you're talking about and he is always telling some tall tale. I wouldn't believe a word he says."

Papa looked puzzled.

"Well, I'm not sure about that. After watching this cyclone tear things up today I wouldn't be surprised at anything they could do. I don't know where to start cleaning up. I'm sure glad it hit the fields and not the house and barn but you're right Slim does like to kid people."

I think the weather where we lived that bothered me most was the wind. That constant and persistent wind that blew almost daily. Once in a while, the wind stopped and then Papa worried about the windmill not turning.

"There hasn't been enough wind to turn the windmill for three days now. The watering troughs are getting low. I hope I don't have to go borrow the water wagon and haul water."

The hills lacked trees to make a wind break and the wind swooped down from over the mountains. This is what caused the wind to blow hot and dry in the summer and in the winter it was freezing cold. In the summer, it picked up dust from the roads or fields and swirled it through the air often causing whirlwinds. In the winter it picked up snow causing blinding conditions through the skies and drifts across the roads.

Board fences built beside the roads broke the wind and kept it from making snowdrifts across the roads. You can still see these fences built to keep back drifting sand or snow in some places along the highways in Idaho.

Sometimes at night, I could hear the wind turning the windmill and making scary sounds that sounded like it might be ghosts screeching and screaming. This frightening sound scared me half out of my wits. Where I slept on a bed in the living room, I could see spooky reflections of the fire flickering through the glass on the door of the potbelly stove. Ghostly looking figures hovered over me and performed weird dances on the walls and ceiling. Suddenly, without any warning, they would even swoop down on my bed.

"Mama! Mama! Can I come in there with you?"

"Come on honey. Did you have a bad dream? Crawl in between Papa and me for a while until it goes away."

The weather also brought some wonderful and joyful days to my life. Waking up in the morning and seeing the first snow of winter falling in big fluffy flakes was always like a gift from heaven for me.

"Look, look, it's snowing for The Baby!"

They always called me The Baby so I guess that is why I called myself The Baby too. This baby name followed me the rest of my life and my family always said, "It's snowing for The Baby" every time it snowed.

One of the wonderful things about winter weather was it brought out the sleds and skis and snowmen popped up everywhere. The whole family pitched in to build snowmen and Rex liked to build snow forts so he could throw snowballs at us.

Then before you hardly knew it the cold winter passed and along came spring. What is so rare as a lovely June morning when the lark in the meadow awakens you with a melody of song? It's time to get up you sleepyhead. Spring brings with it more play time outdoors and more fun on the farm.

Like a knight in shining armor, the golden summer comes bringing even more outdoor fun watching the excitement of harvest time.

Once in a while, on a still summer day, the wind stopped blowing and only slightly rustled the sagebrush. It seemed so peaceful and quiet on those days. Even the quaking aspen grove down by the old house stopped its constant quivering and rested for a while.

One such day comes vividly to mind and I see Papa and me sitting on the bank beside a little mountain brook where pan size brook trout lived. We were just sitting there catching those little buggers as fast as we could pull them out. Mama and my sister were getting our picnic lunch ready while my brother gathered wood to build a fire so Mama could fry the fish. She hollered, "Claude, how soon you wanta' eat?"

Papa took a fish off his hook and hollered back, "We got enough fish now for lunch. We will catch some more later to take home. So anytime you're ready."

Rex's fire was just right for cooking and the big over-size frying pan Mama brought to fry fish in was soon sizzling with bacon grease. Mabel dipped the fish in flour. It wasn't long until the smell of fish, fried spuds and coffee filled the air. It was such a tantalizing smell my stomach started growling.

I did a lot of bragging about how many of the fish I'd caught. No one paid any attention. They just went on talking about what they had been doing and how much fun they were having.

You would have to be there I guess to understand what a wonderful time it was for our family gathered there together enjoying a perfect rest. All the work and worry of farming left back at the farm, forgotten for one glorious day of summer.

Maybe best of all were those sunny warm days with colorful autumn leaves and golden stubble fields. It was called Indian Summer. Once more we looked forward to the winter fun outdoors.

Yes, as I remember those storms, I know it was true that weather played a big role in the way we lived when I was a child. Some of the weather was very nice and some was very bad but with the changing seasons and the whim of the weather we always had a time to have fun outdoors. But to hear them tell about that Thanksgiving Day blizzard in 1922, the day of my birth, you'd think it was the worst weather they ever had.

Chapter 5

Mama used to bake bread every day for the hired men that worked for Papa on the farm. She took the loaves out of the oven and with her bare hands she rubbed the hot tops with freshly churned butter and set them on clean dishtowels to cool. There was always a pan of biscuits too. Even now, I can smell the bread and picture the table with those three lovely loaves of bread shiny from the melted butter. They rest on dishtowels Mama had embroidered with flowers and days of the week. An empty black pan sits near them. It had held all three loaves snuggled side by side when they baked in the Monarch oven.

Cinnamon rolls hot out of the oven full of raisins and sticky with thick brown sugar syrup are in a cast iron skillet close by. The strong smell of cinnamon and sugar floats straight for my nose and the smell is even better than fresh baked bread.

"Mama, I'm hungry."

"You can wait a few minutes. They are too hot now and besides it's almost time for dinner."

"The bread isn't too hot. Can I have the heel with apple butter on it while I'm waiting?"

"No, like I said it would ruin your dinner. You better wait."

Mama's days were filled with many tasks besides the bread making. The garden was another one of these important things that she tended to daily. Mama planted a big garden about a quarter mile from the house. She had to choose a location where the soil held moisture yet had good drainage when we had a cloudburst. Mama and I and walked there every morning to get fresh produce for the noon meal. All the way there, her voice filled the air with songs she learned at church. We marched most of the way singing, 'Onward Christian Soldiers'.

I caught ladybugs in the garden while Mama hoed a few rows every day. I put the cute little bugs on the end of my finger and said, "Ladybug, Ladybug, fly away home. Your house is on fire and your children will burn."

Once in a while the ladybugs just sat there on my finger and fluttered their wings but wouldn't fly home. I got disgusted and decided they didn't care if their children burned or not. I almost cried. Mama got lettuce and peas and other vegetables and I helped carry them back to the house.

Everyone loved Mama's wilted lettuce and she always had to make a big dish full of it. She wilted the lettuce by frying bacon from the slabs of bacon Papa had cured. She then put vinegar and sugar in the bacon grease and poured the hot mixture over the fresh leaf lettuce. Once in a while she added red radishes, cucumbers and little green onions.

Mama kept the lettuce seed from year to year. The original seed came from Switzerland with her family and was handed down from generation to generation. Neighbors still had seeds from this special brown leaf lettuce years later when I visited them after I was grown.

Another task Mama had when the men forgot to do it was carrying the water into the house from the well. The water was pumped out of the well by a tall windmill. The windmill was probably the most important feature on our farm. Sometimes when it broke down or the wind didn't blow for a few days it caused a panic because so many things depended on a steady supply of water.

We had two big watering troughs where the horses and our one cow drank. One day I was playing by one of the troughs by pushing a board around pretending it was a ship. Slim, one of the hired men, said to me, "Did you know if you put a hair from a horse's tail in water it will turn into a snake?"

It wasn't long until I had several potential snakes lined up around the trough and stuck to the edge so the horses wouldn't drink them. Jesse had less hair hanging in her flowing tail after that. I sure hoped I wasn't making any more rattlesnakes. We already had too many of them. I liked the little snakes I saw around the grassy streams in the hills that scurried away when I tried to catch them. There were also lovable little garter snakes in the garden.

I looked for snakes to appear for a couple of weeks and though the horsehairs did get kind of wiry and wiggly I finally gave up. Then I remembered Mama and Papa talking about a man that was a big kidder and I realized that man was Slim our favorite hired man who told me about horsetail snakes. He must have been kidding me.

I watched all day when the men made the frame for the second watering trough. Then they poured cement into the frame. The first trough we had was made from steel and looked like a big bathtub. The horses didn't care which trough they drank from, but I still liked the old one better because I could see my reflection in the shiny bottom.

Rex told me that Helen Keller first associated words with things by putting her hand under the water pump to learn the word water. I often thought of her when I watched the water pouring from the pipe into the troughs. I put my hand under the spout and pretended I was blind and deaf like Helen Keller. I walked through the yard and up on the porch and into the house with my fingers in my ears and my eyes closed. It is very difficult to be blind and deaf I decided as I stumbled on the porch step and tried to find the screen door.

Now, since I am almost deaf and blind, I fully realize what a remarkable and talented person Helen Keller was to be able to overcome such a devastating handicap with the help of her teacher the Miracle Worker. At that time, I never dreamed I would someday have a child that was deaf. My son Bill was left profoundly deaf from meningitis when he was 10 months old but just like Helen his handicap didn't keep him from having a full and remarkable life.

Under the windmill was a rather large building called the well house where Papa kept many wonderful things he used to farm with. I often played with the tools. I especially liked the anvil where he heated irons and horseshoes and things I never knew why or what they were for. I liked the big whetstone I could sit on and pump the pedals to make the wheel go around. I pretended I was riding it like a bicycle. There were curry combs Papa brushed the horses with all full of horse's hair. I played in that building under the windmill a lot because it was cool and so interesting though the smell of oil and grease and drying leather pelts hanging around wasn't very pleasant.

In the well house there were post-hole diggers with two long handles that pulled apart. Papa took me along when he had to put in new fence posts some place.

"You're sure a good little helper. I don't know what I'd do without you here to hand me those staples made special for nailing barbed wire to the post. Before I bought these staples I used to have to bend nails over to fasten the wire. Would you run over to the wagon and bring me the wire cutters out of that wooden box full of tools? I want to cut some of this wire off so I can wrap it around this leaning post that's helping brace up the new post."

Once I heard him say a bad word when he stuck one of the barbs from the wire in his finger.

He said, "Damn it!" I think he learned it from the hired men because I learned that very same word from them. When I said it Mama told me it was a bad word.

Papa jabbed the sharp two ends of the post-hole diggers down in the ground. Then he pushed the handles together and pulled up a lot of dirt. He kept pulling out dirt until he had a hole big enough to set a post. Then he tamped dirt all around the post with the handle of a shovel until the post felt solid when he pushed it.

This must have been hard work because he always pulled out the red bandana he carried in his back pocket, took off his straw hat, and wiped the sweat from his brow and balding head.

"Hop up on the wagon Ruthie, and we'll head for the house and see if Mama's made a pitcher of lemonade."

I could hardly wait to get to the house and the lemonade, "Crack the reins over their backs and make them run Papa!"

"No, we can't do that. They're tired and thirsty too."

When we got close to the house, I could see Mama on the front porch. She had a pitcher of lemonade and two glasses on a tray waiting for us. There was no glass for her because she had still had so much work left to do in her busy day. She knew Papa was hot and tired and she wanted him to rest a bit before he had to start his evening chores. Women in those days were often considered a helpmate and my Mama took that role seriously. She always put the rest of us first though I am sure Papa never thought of her as just a helpmate but as his wife whom he loved very much. I often heard Papa say he was sorry she had so much to do but when he got rich he would make it up to her.

Chapter 6

I had a sister I called Bobel because I couldn't say Mabel and a brother named Rex and I was the baby. I was thirteen years younger than my sister and nine years younger than Rex. My first memories of my sister are that she treated me like a doll to play with. She liked to dress me up and she rocked me and cuddled me. I could feel she loved me very much.

Before we went to town she would catch me, take my blue striped bib overalls off, and scrub me 'til it hurt. She dressed me in a white frilly dress she made for me. The dress was decorated with ribbons shaped into pompoms with streamers that hung from the shoulder to the hem. She sat me at the end of a long oilcloth covered table. I don't know why they called it oilcloth; it didn't have oil on it. Mama bought it at the general store where it hung on a roller and was rolled off and cut to however much she wanted.

I had to sit there on the table until they were ready to go. Bobel didn't want me to get dirty and I didn't dare move. I just sat and swung my legs over the side of the table, twisted at the ribbons and pouted. It seemed like a long time. I think I was very young, maybe not quite three.

I really liked the dresses Mabel made out of big red bandana handkerchiefs. She made us each a dress just alike by sewing two bandanas together and leaving a hole for the neck and arms. She sewed two more on the bottom of hers to make it long enough.

Once Papa had to go to town in a hurry and Mabel didn't have time for the regular ritual of cleaning the dirt off me. When we got to town she put me in the back seat and covered me head to toe with a wool army blanket so people wouldn't see me. We had several of those greenish army blankets from World War I. I suppose you could buy them after the war in government surplus just like after World War II.

Papa shopped at the hardware store for parts for machinery and

Mabel went to the mercantile store. It was a hot summer day. I couldn't breathe under that blanket so I stuck my head out for air.

I heard two women walking on the sidewalk built of boards. The Cuban heels on their shoes made a clunking noise on the boardwalk and they were chattering like the magpies that lived down by the old house in the grove of quaking aspen trees. I peeked out at them. They saw my head sticking out of the blanket and came dashing over sputtering and fuming to rescue me from baking to a crisp under the blanket there in the back seat of Papa's car.

When Mabel came back to the car they bawled her out good for covering me up on such a hot day and leaving me all alone. I must say I agreed with the ladies and I smiled. Then I felt so sorry for myself it almost made me cry when one lady patted my head and said, "Poor child."

As I take these glances back to the years of my childhood I realize how fortunate I was to have the brother and sister and mother and father that I had. I guess they spoiled me rotten in the eyes of some people. I hear the phrase dysfunctional families so often now and it breaks my heart. Families with fathers and mothers and brothers and sisters are such a wonderful way of life and so different from single parents with single children. I can say this from personal experience.

Mama didn't believe in spanking children as a way of punishment.

"You don't spoil children by being good to them. You spoil them by being mean to them and that makes them want to be mean. Spanking is mean."

Still most families seemed to go by the rule spare the rod and spoil the child and now when people describe the spankings they had as children they often sound more like beatings to me. These people seem rather proud of receiving such harsh discipline and usually say they deserved it.

I do remember getting two spankings although I guess I could hardly call them spankings. They made such an impression I never needed another one. Once by Papa when a friend and I conspired to take a dime from her sister's purse and once by Mama when she got really worried when I was late coming home from school because I went downtown. The punishments were such dramatic occasions that I never dared to chance it again.

Papa made it a big deal by making me wait until he went out on the ditch bank and cut a willow. It was a long wait. I don't know why he was gone so long. The tension built up. I got really scared. I had never had Papa get so upset with me before. He usually laughed at whatever I did. I begged Mama to hide me so he couldn't find me.

"No, I can't do that."

Now I'm trying to remember being even touched with the willow and I can't. Maybe he just didn't have the heart to use it.

I don't have any trouble remembering Mama and her willow. When she caught up with me she wrapped it around my legs all the way home from downtown. Of course, I had long stockings on and didn't even feel the switching but I don't think anything has ever embarrassed me as much in my whole life. I can see myself trying to keep from crying because of the people who were staring at us. I see Mama with that silly willow clutched in her hand and a look in her eyes I had never seen before. It was hard to tell what she was thinking. The embarrassment hurt me far worse than the sting of the willow.

Rex and Mabel played a large part in my growing up and their influence was pretty much a plus for me. Mabel was like a second mother. She made my clothes and taught me about things I needed to know and took care of my needs and wants. I was always her darling baby sister even after I was grown.

Years piled up behind us and it seems we grew apart until we weren't as close as during those tender years of my early life. Our interests took different directions as we aged. Different religions, different political views, totally different ways of life and we lived far away from each other in different states. Some of her children were closer to my age than she was. I've noticed in my later life that siblings often seem to have differences after they are older and some even become quite hostile in their feelings toward each other especially after a death in the family. This seems strange.

Mama used to say, "My three kids are as different as night and day," and I agree.

Mabel and I thought Rex was Mama's favorite.

My sister did a lot of my talking for me. If someone asked me a question, she would answer while I shyly ducked my head and I often heard such words as:

"You don't talk very much Ruthie. What's the matter? The cat got your tongue?"

Why did grown-ups always ask me that? It made me worry the cat might really try to get my tongue.

While Mabel was in high hchool, she became very ill with what they called Saint Vitus Dance in those days. I don't remember a thing about it but Mama told me we moved to Oregon for a short time to take Mabel to a doctor that knew how to treat her illness. We stayed in The Dalles for several months. I'm not sure if Mabel ever graduated from high school. Another winter we lived in Rexburg to be close to a doctor and I don't remember that either. The effects of St. Vitus Dance plagued her for many years. Her illness made her interested in helping people that were ill and later she went into nursing.

During her lifetime, she helped lots of people through tough problems. She was a very compassionate, caring and giving person. Once she took a boy with troubles in and he became a member of her family just as surely as if he had actually been born into it. I don't know his name because everyone called him Duck, and I don't know why they called him Duck.

My brother Rex was my hero and I adored him in spite of his teasing that kept me bawling a lot. I grew up with what they used to call an inferiority complex and extreme shyness. I never hear that expression any more. Maybe no one feels inferior nowadays. I finally grew out of it, but for years I blamed Rex for my inferior feelings and my shyness because he teased me so much.

"You only got one freckle and it starts at the end of your nose and goes all over your face. You'd be a lot taller if so much of you hadn't turned up for feet. Tattle tale tattle tale hanging by a bull's tail."

Rex taught me things I needed to know about horses and ermine traps and beavers and fishing and sled dogs and how to be a tomboy that enjoyed doing the same things he did. It helped make balance in my life to have so many different interests. I must say I have done many things in my life that are not usually things women were destined to do in the past and lots of women wouldn't think of doing nowadays.

Sitting in the row of horseradish in the dress Mabel made
for me

On the swing Papa built me and the bummer lamb the
sheepherders gave me

Barefooted in my coveralls
looking for a lost marble

Mama and Papa and me at the farm

Papa and Mabel

Papa and me

Chapter 7

The meals we had when we lived on our farm were so different from the way we eat now. We had our big meals for breakfast and for lunch. We called lunch dinner. Our evening meal we called supper and sometimes it was very light except during harvest when there were more hired men.

Thick slices of bread spread with apple butter and glasses of milk or buttermilk from the butter Mama had churned that day. Sometimes we had pancakes with thick cream and sugar on them. Mama made syrup by boiling brown sugar and putting maple flavoring in it. A piece of pie made from Mama's canned peaches or from huckleberries that grew in the hills by our farm. There were always chokecherry jellies to spread on the bread. Chokecherries grew down by the old house. Devil's Food Cake with white frosting Mama made with egg whites often showed up on the table. Cookies of every kind, oatmeal cookies bursting with walnuts and raisins and sugar cookies sprinkled with sugar. My favorite cookies were filled cookies made with a thickened raisin filling in the inside.

One time when we were picking chokecherries by the old house to make jelly, a big black bear started picking berries on the other side of the bush. Mama threw our berries down and grabbed my hand. We ran for the house as fast as our legs could carry us.

"Papa! Papa! We saw a bear! He was big and black and Mama screamed. We ran as fast as we could. Will he come in the house after us? What should we do?"

"Just calm down, Ruthie. No, he won't come in the house. Mama probably scared him away. I'll go see about Mr. Bear."

Papa went looking for the bear with a gun but Mr. Bear must have left the country when he heard Mama screaming and we never saw him again. Papa thought the bear had wandered over the mountain from Yellowstone Park.

After supper, I looked up on the hill to see if the coyote was still up there watching me. He always was.

Mama checked the kerosene lamps to see if there was enough coal oil in them. She trimmed the wicks and wiped the black soot from inside the glass chimneys with a piece of newspaper. We had one gasoline lantern that made a much brighter light. We seldom used the lamps in the summer because we got up with the sun and went to bed with the sun.

On hot nights we climbed on top of the haystack and made our beds up there under the stars. It was so cozy between Mama and Papa. The summer nights were wonderful with a soft cool breeze carrying the perfumes of the hay and wheat fields. The cow mooed her contented moo and a horse whinnied back as though he was saying, "Me too."

Papa told stories of Oregon.

"It never got this hot in Oregon. The breeze from the ocean kept the days and nights just a nice temperature. Everything is so green in Oregon because of the rain. It rains often and a lot. They raise different crops like what's in Mama's garden for people to eat. There are trees everywhere. Huge trees so big around you can't reach around them. Enough trees to last forever."

Papa had no idea that demand and modern ways of logging in Oregon would deplete the forests until there wouldn't be enough to last forever.

Papa never seemed to tire of answering my questions.

"What's an ocean?"

"An ocean is so much water that you can see it as far away as where the sky touches ground and where the sun goes to bed at night. People build boats like the one we go fishing in only as big as the barn and sail away to other countries and see people that look lots different than we do. We don't have many people here in Idaho from other countries so I guess you have never seen anyone from another country that looks any different than we do."

Mama said, "Tell her about the hop yards near Salem where I won the championship for picking the most hops. I never worked so hard in my life. Even here I get to rest once in a while. Now you two go to sleep."

That became my dream. I dreamed of growing up and moving to Oregon.

There are still hop fields just outside Salem, Oregon where my parents picked hops about a hundred or so years ago. I have pictures of the hop pickers of that time. Hops are used to flavor beer and I heard that most of them are now grown in Oregon for this purpose.

During the night the lonely sound of a coyote's howl echoed through the hills and I felt happy to be between Papa and Mama high on top of the haystack where he couldn't reach me.

Papa was encouraged by his sister Edna, her husband Philip and their friends Ernest and Dolly to move to Idaho. They had moved there a couple of years before my folks and settled on dry farms. Aunt Ed and Uncle Philip had a really nice house. Dolly and Ernest's place wasn't as nice but it was a whole lot nicer than the ramshackle farmhouse we lived in.

One day while we were visiting Aunt Ed there was a lighting storm raging through the countryside. Lightning was striking all around followed by tremendously loud claps of thunder. Mabel seemed to enjoy standing by the door watching but I hid behind Mama's chair and covered my ears.

A crank telephone hung on the wall beside Mabel. Suddenly a bolt of lightning made the phone ring as it came through the phone. It knocked Mabel halfway across the room. Mabel was badly hurt and it was a long time before she recovered. The doctor said she was lucky to be alive.

Chapter 8

Papa had moved the family to Idaho to seek his fortune. I think his plan was to become a very wealthy farmer. Land was cheap and easy to get. Papa leased his thousand acres from Fess Fuller and C.C. Moore who were realtor partners. C.C. Moore was the former governor of Idaho. The Moores visited us often to check the crops on his investment property and they became our very close friends.

Governor Moore had a habit of walking in without knocking. Of course, in those days a lot of our friends never knocked but just opened the door and looked in.

"Hello, anybody home?"

I can't imagine that now when we keep our doors locked day and night. Intruders break the doors open anyway to rob and our lives are often threatened by people with guns.

Our kitchen stove stood out from the wall making room behind it to set the galvanized washtub so we could bathe in the warmth of the stove. It wasn't very private and Governor Moore walked in on Mama bathing one day.

"Hello, anybody home?"

Mama screamed so I could hear her clear out by the well house and she was so upset she really gave him a piece of her mind.

I heard her say, "From now on I want you to knock when you come to see us."

I pondered whether to run and find Papa or go see what was going on. I couldn't decide which so I didn't do anything.

Papa saw Governor Moore's car parked by the road and came running from the barn right past me to see what all the screaming was about. I guess everyone felt embarrassed. Governor Moore left immediately. There was a big cloud of dust following behind his fancy touring car as he sped away.

When I was about three or four, the Moores sometimes took me home with them to stay for a week. They had no children of their own so I suppose they enjoyed having a child around even a little girl tomboy like me.

Mrs. Moore dressed me up in cute little girl clothes until I passed for their idea of what a little girl should look like. I liked all the fuss they made over me but I usually got homesick in a couple of days and they would have to take me home long before a week passed.

The Moores lived in a beautiful big brick house in St. Anthony, one of the many small towns around that area where our farm was located. At least it seemed beautiful and big to me. They even had oriental rugs on the floors and indoor plumbing.

I was fascinated by the bathroom. At home we had a privy outside a gate and down a long path behind the house. That outhouse stunk to high heaven and it penetrated the air in the summer until we went to town and got a sack of lime and put in it.

In the winter, it was a long cold walk in the snow. I had to put on my overshoes but could never take time to buckle the buckles and they flip flopped and caught together and made me trip and fall in the snow.

No matter how hard I tried I couldn't keep from peering down at that disgusting sight below every time I went in there.

I unbuttoned the flap in the seat of my coveralls and sat on the hard seat. Papa cut one of the holes just my size. If someone forgot to shut the door as they came out snow blew in and I had to brush it off and sit on the icy cold seat.

We really did have Montgomery Ward and Sears and Roebuck catalogues we used for paper sometimes. There was a moon shape cut out near the roof of the outhouse to let in air and light.

I didn't like to go out there at night. It was darker than a stack of black cats. Beside my bed sat an ornate porcelain chamber I could use at night. Mama called it the slop jar. Sometimes I snuck in there to use the pot during the daytime and Mama didn't like me doing that one little bit.

"If you do that one more time I'll make you go empty it."

I didn't know which was worse, emptying the pot or going out to the privy.

Every time the Moores took me home with them they stopped in

Ashton on our way to St. Anthony and we went into a drug store for treats.

"What would you like to drink Ruthie?"

"I'll have a Green River."

Green River was a soda fountain drink of that time. I don't seem to remember that it had a particular flavor only that it was sweet and I liked the name Green River. It sounded better than orange crush.

Drug stores all had these wonderful counters with marble tops and stools to sit on where you could order anything from ice cream sundaes to banana splits or my favorite, strawberry ice cream sodas.

After I finished the Green River, Mr. Moore bought me a Baby Ruth candy bar. He knew Baby Ruth was my favorite because it had my name. Candy bars were smaller at that time and only cost a nickel. There was even a smaller version that cost a penny.

We sat at a little round metal table with a marble top on little round metal chairs with curved legs and lots of fancy metal work on the back. That's where I ate my Baby Ruth and drank my Green River.

I could see the glass enclosed candy case with boxes of penny candy lined up in a row. Jawbreakers, all day suckers, licorice sticks shaped like cigars, peppermint sticks, gumballs, horehound, and only a penny each.

Mr. Moore must have read my mind, "Get another piece of candy if you want to."

The man squatted behind the counter to reach the candy inside. I couldn't decide which one to choose.

"I think I'll take an all-day sucker."

"Which one?"

"The red one."

He started to get up with the red sucker.

"No, wait a minute. Is that one grape? I like grape better." He started to hand me the grape sucker.

"I've changed my mind. I think I'll get the licorice stick with the cigar band on it. "

I just remembered my sister never let me have licorice. She didn't like for me to get all messy with it and now that she wasn't here it was my chance. I loved licorice.

He put the grape sucker back and got the licorice.

Mrs. Moore got up and walked over to the counter.

"I don't think she should have licorice. She's so messy with it. Choose something else Ruthie."

I looked at the choices a long time. I couldn't decide which candy I wanted. The man was still squatting waiting for me. He was kind of fat. It sounded like he grunted but I guess he was just getting short of breath from all the exercise.

"Well, for crying out loud, hurry up and make up your mind. These old knees can't take much more of this squatting and getting up and down."

Mr. Moore started laughing and came over to the counter, "Give her one of everything in there. Come on Ruthie, we got to be on our way."

I had often dreamed of being in that drug store. In my dreams I helped myself to anything I wanted. My dreams had come true! When I left the store with the Moores I had one every kind of candy in the showcase in a candy sack with the top twisted and held tightly in my hand. I carried it everywhere I went and it lasted nearly a week.

We usually had homemade everything including our candy. Mama and Papa made taffy from a recipe they had gotten from a candy store in Oregon. Mama boiled the sugar syrup until it bubbled and cracked and popped. She held the spoon high over the kettle and when it made a thread from the spoon to the kettle she knew it was ready to pull. Then she poured it on a big turkey platter smeared with butter. While it was still too hot to handle she and Papa picked it up on taffy hooks, big metal hooks that look kind of like a hay hook, and they pulled it back and forth across the room between the two of them. When it turned from yellow to white and reached the perfect stage they took it to the table and broke it in pieces by hitting it with the handle of the butcher knife. It was such a treat with big chewy pieces full of air holes caused by the way they pulled the candy across the room back and forth for a long time.

Years later Mama was offered twenty-five dollars for that recipe so she sold it to a delicatessen. I have a copy but I think it has something left out because I could never get it to turn out like her taffy. I've never seen taffy like that was except when my sister made it. It was nothing like the saltwater taffy we buy every time we go to the coast.

Chapter 9

My parents always had fun even though they worked hard. They often went to the dances at Warm River Dance Hall on Saturday nights.

I have this wonderful video-like memory of Papa standing in front of the washstand in the kitchen, getting ready to go to the dance. There is a mirror with Papa's reflection hanging above the washstand. His face is covered with lather from his shaving brush that he dips in his shaving cup. A big wash pan full of steaming water sits on the washstand. He strops his straight edge razor on a leather strop that hangs from the wall. He sings funny little ditties of love and joy. Every now and then he throws in a dance step or two. He starts singing,

"Gonna dance off both of my shoes when they play the jelly roll blues."

I thought my Papa was such a brave man. I had been warned many times not to touch that razor.

"It's very sharp and it will cut your fingers off."

Yet here was Papa scraping that sharp dangerous thing down across his face and back up across his throat. He pulled his nose up with his other hand and twisted his face to one side and shaved his upper lip. It took a particular skill to get the whiskers out of that hole in his chin. There was a big dimple in his chin and I always think of Papa when I see Kirk Douglas as he has a cleft chin just like Papa's.

Occasionally that razor did nick him and he stuck little pieces of tobacco paper on the nicks to stop the bleeding. It looked funny but everything about watching my Papa shave was fascinating to me as I gazed up at him in admiration.

My brother Rex inherited his great dimple but my sister and I only inherited his fine thin balding hair.

Papa was six foot two. He looks taller in my pictures of him so maybe he was. He looked so handsome in his white shirt Mama had just ironed for him. She had to heat up the flat irons on the cook stove but it was a labor of love.

Mama then heated the curling iron in the chimney of the kerosene lamp to curl her newly bobbed hair. Papa emptied the washtub of bath water twice for them and once for me. I think we looked nice even though it was such an effort.

Nowadays it doesn't take so much effort to dress up to go out. I wonder why some people don't. My parents had to carry in buckets of water and heat it on the stove and take turns bathing in the washtub every time they went any place. It was hard work getting their clothes washed and ironed or pressed. Nowadays, I only buy wash and wear that doesn't need ironing.

Papa and Mama took me to the dances with them. People piled their coats on the stage behind the musicians and when the kids got tired and sleepy they climbed up on the coats and went to sleep worn out from running, playing, dancing and having fun. We fell asleep while the banjos and fiddles and piano were still pounding away in our ears.

Papa always danced with me and taught me how to follow him in the beautiful waltz steps. I've always loved to dance. It doesn't look like much fun when I watch dancers on TV now just moving around but not really dancing. They had such intricate steps back in those years of my life and kids learned to dance from going to the dances with their parents. Two Step. Virginia Reel. Waltz. Charleston. Square Dances.

When we got home from the dances I always pretended to be asleep so Papa would carry me in the house. We both knew I wasn't asleep but I think he enjoyed the game as much as I did. I could tell from the way he kissed me and tucked me in, "Goodnight my little angel."

Sometimes we went to the neighbors for parties on holidays or birthdays. There was good old-fashioned music with fiddles, banjos, washboards even a Jews Harp. My brother played the saxophone and clarinet. "Yes sir, that's my baby. No sir, don't mean maybe."

There was always plenty of food furnished by the women. Cakes, pies, sandwiches made with headcheese. Headcheese was made from the meat on the head of a hog. It was cooked until it made kind of a jelly from the juices and then was formed into loaves they could slice. Cottage cheese was made by setting a pan of sour milk on the back of the stove until it curdled and then draining off the water and pouring thick cream in it.

One of Mama's specialties was chicken and dumplings.

"Come and help your brother catch those two old Rhode Island Red hens. They quit laying eggs so I think I'll make chicken and dumplings to take to the potluck at the Browns'. The Plymouth Rock baby chickens have finally got old enough to start laying so while you are out by the hen house see if there are any eggs."

Rex started bossing the job of catching hens. He gave me the hardest job.

"You shoo them over by the corner of the fence and I'll catch them when we get them cornered."

The hens must have caught on to the plan and one ran one way and one the other. In fact, they ran for several minutes in every direction except in the corner. Mama came and caught them both all by herself but I think they just got tired of running.

Mama held them by their legs and wings and chopped their heads off on the chopping block where Papa split wood. They flopped around a while then she dipped them in a bucket of scalding water, plucked the feathers off and put them on to boil. People always thought Mama's chicken and dumplings were extra special. I don't know what she did different but I have never had any that even remotely compared to hers. I guess maybe it's because she didn't use biscuit mix to make the dumplings.

Every Fourth of July we had a big picnic at Warm River with friends and relatives. There were watermelons cooling in the river while women cooked the fish the men had caught. The men were busy turning the handle on the ice cream freezer. Kids shot off firecrackers and cap guns and the hill across the river echoed with the sounds of people celebrating Fourth of July. After dark, there were more spectacular fireworks. They shot up high in the sky and rained down in bright colors. We screamed with delight as each rocket filled the night with colored sparkles.

Papa brought the ice to make ice cream. It was from a big bank of drifted snow on which Papa had piled thick layers of straw. The straw kept the snow from melting and it turned into ice. The snow bank provided ice all summer for our icebox. Papa always knew how to make do with what he had.

Electricity did not extend out as far as our place in those days and so we lived in a time zone that dated far back into the pioneer days when everything had to be done the hard way. Still I wonder if life wasn't appreciated more and family fun was more entertaining than what we have nowadays.

It seems to me people don't enjoy their beautiful homes as much as we did that ramshackle old farm house and they go outside the home in search of entertainment. Their garages are so full of things they buy they have to park their cars in the driveway and on the street. Our neighbors didn't live next door but we knew them for miles around and enjoyed good times and friendships with them in our homes.

Now we have the most recent gadgets to cook with but often eat out. There is usually a waiting line it is so crowded. I watch people eating. I can't tell if they are enjoying the food and the other person's company from the way they look. I seldom see them talking or laughing. There is no expression, but only a kind of glum isolated stare as though their thoughts focus entirely on themselves.

I wonder, "Has the home become just a place to sleep and to store all the junk we buy?"

It almost seems children spend more time with babysitters than with their parents. Children are so smart now they are like little adults and the innocent play of just being a child has been replaced by too much knowledge and too many things at too young an age.

Perhaps back in the old days, before computers, when children used make believe in their play they stayed children longer. Now with computers and technology, children become adults too quickly. A child isn't really a child anymore.

Wouldn't it be more natural to develop in their own imaginary world as a child using imaginary toys with the objects around that interest them and not with adult ideas and toys long before its time to be an adult? I don't know the answer. Things and times change and always have. I remember parents from the good old days thought almost the same things about my generation.

Chapter 10

Papa went fishing in the Teton River, which flowed behind the farm. He had to climb down a very steep embankment. The fish were so big they hung from his hand to the ground. A nice big fat rainbow trout is very lovely to look at. They were so heavy it was hard for him to carry two of them back up the steep cliff. Mama and I waited for him at the top. We watched for his head to pop up over the bank and when we saw that big grin on his face we knew the fish were biting that day.

Before Papa went fishing he always had me help him catch the grasshoppers he used for bait. There was a rocky piece of ground we couldn't cultivate that was full of June Grass and the grasshoppers must have thought it was their special place as there were hundreds of them living there.

We caught them on the ground by slapping our straw hats over them. When we picked them up they spit tobacco juice all over our hand. Yuck. It was such a nasty job but Papa needed my help and that made me feel important. I hurried to stuff them in the Sir Walter Raleigh tobacco can. I had to be fast to keep the other grasshoppers from jumping out before I got the lid closed.

I grew up loving to feel the tug of a pan size trout on the end of my line. The thrill of finally getting him reeled in to shore and having Papa dip him up with a net followed me well into middle age. I can proudly say I seldom went fishing that I didn't catch my limit. My limit was only one fish so it easy for me to catch my limit.

That is a lie or rather a joke. I have often caught the legal limit on my many fishing trips during my life.

Empty tobacco cans were such useful items for us. Because of their flat shape, they just fit in the little pocket at the top of Papa's bib overalls so they made a handy bait box. They were also good for holding crayons or marbles or ladybugs or other important things I needed to keep track of. I had several cans full of my treasures in my orange crate stand that stood by my bed. In those days oranges came in a wooden box that had a partition in the middle. If you stood the box on end it could be used as a nightstand with a shelf and it had many other uses. The stores used them for boxing groceries sometimes so we had lots of them.

The hired men used loose tobacco in the cans to roll cigarettes. They tapped the can with one finger and the tobacco spilled out into a little paper they held folded in the other hand. They rolled it up and ran their tongue along the edge of the paper to seal it. They struck a match on the seat of their pants or their thumbnail and lit fire to the cigarette. They puffed on it until it glowed red giving them great enjoyment it seemed by the looks on their faces.

The smoke curled around their heads or floated up in little rings when they puckered their lips into a circle and opened their mouths. They sat around in the yard relaxing on blocks of wood after supper. I sat in my swing and watched the men smoking and listened to them talking. That's how I learned about some things my parents had never told me about and probably didn't want me to know. Often they sang songs about lonely cowboys while one real cowboy strummed on a guitar.

Sometimes they used Bull Durham tobacco that came in little bags with a drawstring. Those bags were especially useful for marbles and fit my pocket much better than the tobacco cans. When the men first came to work Papa always told them "No smoking or cussing around the women!"

But sometimes I heard some pretty strong words coming from the barn. The way it sounded some of those horses were pretty stubborn. The cow got cussed too when she managed to kick even with her hobbles on.

Besides the fresh fish we always had wild meat. Mama canned lots of meat in a big copper boiler. She filled mason jars with the meat. She set them in the copper boiler and covered them with water. Then she boiled them for hours. When she opened a jar of the meat for dinner, she made gravy on it. That is still one of my favorite memories of all the good food we ate in those days of plenty on the farm, especially the canned venison.

Along with the uncommon foods that were common to us, we had weeds that we ate every spring that Mama called our spring tonic. These lowly weeds were pigweed and dandelion greens and it makes my mouth water thinking about them.

Our dandelions had big tender leaves not at all like the dandelions here in Oregon and they looked good enough to eat. The pigweed had red stems and I've never seen it any place but Idaho. Mama cooked the wild greens like she did spinach and served them with vinegar and sugar and sliced hard boiled eggs on top. I think this way of preparing greens came from the Swiss German side of her family.

Another weed we used to gather on the ditch banks and along the fencerows where it grew wild on irrigated land several miles from the dry farm was wild asparagus. We canned it for winter, but I didn't think it tasted as good as when it was freshly picked.

Mama told me about taking me to a cafe when I was very little.

"Do you want a hamburger or hot dog?"

"No, I want moose meat."

I don't think I knew what a hamburger was. I don't know if there were hunting seasons in those days out where we lived. I just know we had lots of deer and elk and moose to eat.

Just like the pioneers, my family hunted for food and not for the thrill of the hunt or for trophies. In fact Papa was so soft-hearted I think it was very difficult for him to look at one of those animals in the woods and then shoot it while they stood and looked back at him. I still feel the pity I had for animals when I saw the men pull them up to hang while they gutted them and cleaned them. I ran for the house.

Even now when I see a wild animal's glass eyes peering at me from a wall where the trophy head is hanging the vision of a dead deer hanging from a frame at the farm or a tree in the woods comes to my mind.

Chapter 11

The old saying a man may work from sun to sun but a woman's work is never done really describes Mama's life on the farm. I have mentioned before that there was always so much hard work for her. I think she enjoyed being busy because she did most of her work while she sang a song. She seemed happy with her life.

I remember her washing clothes in the old wooden washing machine. First Mama boiled the whites in the copper boiler poking them around with an old broom handle cut for that purpose. Then she lifted them out of the boiling water with the broom handle and into the machine. She pulled a wooden handle on the machine back and forth to agitate the clothes. Next, the wet clothes were poked through a hand turned wringer attached to the washer to squeeze the water out. I have seen a few of these old wooden washing machines in museums and they always take me back to those smells of clothes and soap when Mama did a washing. The wonderful smell of clothes, when I helped Mama take them off the clothesline after they had hung in the sun and fluttered in the breeze all day.

Then there was the ironing she did by heating flat irons on the stove. There was a detachable handle and she could change a cold iron for a hot iron. Everything had to be ironed, even the dishtowels she made from the twenty-five pound sacks the flour came in. She didn't have an ironing board like we use now. Hers was just a wide board with a cover wrapped around it and placed between the backs of two chairs.

She mended clothes on a treadle sewing machine. Her feet went up and down on the foot pedal causing a belt to turn that made the needle go up and down through the cloth. When the Levis or shirts couldn't be mended any longer she made other useful items with them such as pot holders or braided rugs. Even the hired men asked her to mend a shirt, sew a button on, or iron something for them.

She cooked for about ten men during the hot harvest season with no electricity and no air conditioner. Maybe not that many men but it seemed like that to me when I think about the long table across our kitchen full of men.

Mama always had the floor freshly scrubbed when I got up in the morning. She scrubbed by pouring a bucket of sudsy water on the floor. The suds were made with a bar of soap she made with lard or bacon drippings and lye. Sometimes she bought bars of Fels-Naptha soap. She swept the sudsy water out the door with the broom. It took half a day for the wood floor to dry but the smell of the boards and soap were such a clean smell it still lingers among my best memories of the farm. I loved that house but when I see pictures of it now I wonder how we ever lived in it.

Our house was a ramshackle old farmhouse. Inside the house there were slats nailed on the walls and lined with a heavy grayish colored paper called felt paper. It seemed a little like cloth so it may have had cloth fiber in it. Mama put fresh calcimine of bright yellow, pink, or blue over the paper every year to cover the fly specks. I don't know exactly what calcimine is.

Mama sprayed an insect spray from a metal can with a hand pump and there were ribbons of sticky flypaper that the flies stuck to that she hung from the ceiling. Mama purchased these items from the Raleigh man or the Watkins man who used to come past the farm with spices and vanilla and pudding mixes. We often had peddlers that brought fresh fruit or household goods too. Mama thought some of their wares were much better than she could buy at the general store in Drummond.

She gave us a dose of Watkins liniment when we got the summer complaint from eating too much fresh fruit and it seemed to work. Years later I made her take a dose of her own medicine when she got an upset stomach.

"Oh, that is so terrible I'm sorry I ever made you take it."

It was the first time she ever tasted it.

This reminds me of another of her favorite remedies. At the first sign of a cough or sniffle she fried a big skillet of onions and made an onion poultice that she wrapped in a warm towel and placed on the chest of the offender, usually me. It was supposed to draw out the inflammation. I'm not sure if it did but I survived the treatment.

Some thirty or forty years later my sister wrote a letter telling me she had just gotten over a terrible bout with the flu.

"I've never been so sick in my life and I just couldn't seem to get over it. I tried everything. I thought of Mama's onion poultices. I cut up a couple onions and fried them until they glazed and turned a golden brown. They looked so good and smelled heavenly so I decided to eat them. And you know I think they did just as much good in my tummy as they would have on my chest."

Castor oil was another thing Mama had never tasted or she would have been sorry she ever made me take that horrible laxative with the juice of an orange. All my life when I drink orange juice I imagine I can taste castor oil. Kids nowadays do not know how lucky they are. I don't think they've ever heard of castor oil.

On the backside of our ramshackle old house someone had built a big lean to. Mama fixed it up so our two hired men could sleep there and have a place of their own to spend time and keep their belongings.

It was really quite cozy and I liked to go in there and snoop through their things. They had many interesting items that fascinated me. They kept their personal chaps, saddles and spurs there. The room had a funny smell. It stunk.

One day I saw a little bottle up on top of a cupboard where they hung clothes. I stood on a chair and took it down. I thought it was just great the way it rolled around when I poured some silvery stuff out of it onto the bed. I lifted the quilt a little and it rolled in to a puddle of little beads. I rolled those beads all over the bed just to watch them huddle back together. I got into trouble over that but I suppose mercury isn't a good toy for a child.

The men used the mercury when they panned for gold. I found this out when Mama explained why I had been bad and should never go in the bunkhouse again.

Chapter 12

I wonder why we lived in the house where there were no trees and no green lawn when there was another house on our farm that was nestled in a grove of quaking aspen trees. A cool breeze kept the aspen leaves glistening and shimmering in the sunlight that filtered through to the ground. They danced constantly to the tunes the wind whistled. Willows, chokecherry bushes and a berry called Haws that I really liked grew close by. I liked to go there with Mama to pick berries and just enjoy that delightful place where it seemed so cool and peaceful.

Mama let me take my straw hat off in the shade down by the old house and it felt wonderful with my hat off in the breeze. Every spring the whole family got a new straw hat to wear in the blistering sun of summer. Mama never let me out the door without my hat because I had very fair skin and freckles. They called me a toe head because of my white hair.

The old house was about a quarter mile from the house we lived in. Both houses were built with lodgepole pine like the logs Papa brought down from Island Park where he went to get our firewood or fence posts. The logs had been hewn flat on two sides and notched at the ends to make them fit snug. I think both houses were built many years before we lived there. Actually, the house we lived in had a newer addition built on to the log part. The new addition had regular house boards.

For a couple of years Mama dug up little aspen trees down by the old house and planted them around our yard. She carried bucket after bucket of water from the well house and kept the trees watered almost daily but the trees died anyway. Our yard baked hard as cement and only troublesome puncture weeds could survive there.

I suppose that horrible weed called puncture weed was called that because it could puncture tires. It got my bare feet if I wasn't careful and made a painful puncture. Between ticks and stickers I was always getting something pulled out of me. Mama put turpentine on the ticks to make them back out. They were usually on the back of my neck and they got so full of my blood it made them about twice their actual size. People get Rocky Mountain Fever from ticks but I guess none of us ever did.

Shooting Stars that some people called bird's bills bloomed by the old house and Johnnie jump ups called buttercups in Oregon jumped up at the first sight of spring. We had a different flower though that really looked like a cup of butter.

There by the old house seemed like such a wonderful place where fairies might live and I always wished we lived there instead of the pigs. I'm not sure how many pigs lived in such luxury but in my memory I can see a lot of pigs. A nice little spring probably bubbled up there because I remember the mud puddle where Papa's pigs wallowed in the mud. They rooted around in the yard digging up roots with their snouts.

I liked to chase the little pigs and make them run and squeal until their mother stopped rooting and looked up at me with an evil eye, her mouth still chewing something juicy that oozed from her big jaw. One side of her was usually covered with dried caked mud. I wondered how the little pigs ever got their dinner when she laid down so they could suck. She looked so dirty and mean. The old boar hog was kept penned up in a pigpen. He watched me too with evil eyes and grunted loud painful sounding grunts. I was afraid he wanted out so he could eat me.

The neighbors started calling our place Hog Hollow pronounced Hog Holler because of the pigs. The last time I visited that area there was a road sign about a mile away where we used to have our mailbox with the words, Hog Hollow RD. It is now the official name for that road and is on the map of Idaho.

A few years ago my son and granddaughter and I visited all the places in Idaho where I spent the first years of my life. We stopped in Boise to get some pamphlets at the information center before we started our tour. The pamphlet said they didn't know how Hog Hollow got its name but they thought it was from the razor back mountains around there. I like my true version better.

When my son, granddaughter and I arrived at Hog Hollow, the

only thing remaining where our home had been on our dry farm was some cement rubble. It was in a pile a few feet back from the road, surrounded by a cultivated field where our well house and windmill were. I knew the cement pile must have been from the watering trough I watched the hired men make. Nearby we found a horseshoe, which had to be from one of our horses, because horses were replaced by gasoline-powered machinery after we left the farm. We brought it home and mounted it on a board and it now hangs in our family room. The horseshoe still has the rust and dirt from the farm on it.

Chapter 13

Papa raised wheat and certified seed potatoes on our dry farm. The potatoes were raised without the benefit of irrigation so they didn't get very big. The seed potatoes were called 'one drops' because one whole potato was all you needed to plant each hill. They were treated with blue vitro to keep out bugs and rot. The potatoes Papa grew were an experiment by The Bureau of Agriculture for growing seed potatoes. Now Idaho furnishes most of the seed potatoes that are sold all over the world.

Harvest was an important time on the farm. The neighbors helped each other and besides there were extra hired men. The grain was harvested with a combine pulled by ten horses. I think ten. I can't remember for sure. Combines were a big machine with a long wheel with paddles on it that pulled the grain back into the machine as the paddles turned. It was driven by a long belt powered by the wheels turning on the ground as the combine was pulled across the field by the horses. The heads of the grain were cut off leaving chaff and straw. The grain was then separated from all this and poured into gunnysacks hanging to catch it where it came out after the separation. A man then sewed the tops of the sacks with a big needle and twine. He twisted the corners of the sack into ears and wrapped the twine around them. It gave the men something to hold onto when they lifted them up on the wagon.

My uncle had a grain elevator on his farm where he poured the loose grain to save until he got a good price. My cousin Harold and I liked to play in the grain by running around fast enough to keep from sinking down in it. But that soon ended when we got caught.

"For crying out loud you kids should know better than that. If you sunk down in the grain you would smother and we wouldn't even know what became of you!"

I played on the combine when it wasn't in use. Sometimes it was a big ship and I sailed away on the ocean in Oregon that Papa often told me about. Or, it was a mansion and I was the rich lady that lived in it. Sometimes, it was a schoolhouse where I taught school. It had lots of different areas and little stairs that led to them so it was fun just climbing around. Once I found a little can. I opened it and took a whiff. It was terrible.

"Papa what is that stuff in that can in the tool box by the seat on the combine? I opened the lid to see what it was and it really smells funny. It made me feel sick. Kind of like when I went to the hospital to get my tonsils out."

Mama threw up her hands like she always did when she got upset with something I did.

"Land of Goshen child! How many times do I have to tell you to quit snooping into everything? I wish you would stay away from the machinery and quit climbing around on the combine. There's stuff all over the place you could get hurt on. I can't keep my eye on you every minute."

She turned to Papa then and said, "I wish you would watch her closer when she's out there with you."

Papa told me it was ether and for me to leave it alone. I don't know what ether was used for on the combine.

My brother teased me, and as I said before I bawled a lot, but sometimes he would play with me. Of course, he was about fourteen or fifteen before I was very big. He decided we should dig a tunnel in the field behind the house. I thought this was great just having him pay attention to me and we worked very hard digging a really big hole.

Digging a tunnel is a hard dirty job and besides it is scary under the ground. Papa didn't know about our tunnel and when they cut the wheat the combine fell in it and was 'broke down' preventing any harvesting for several days. This was serious as it affected the neighbors' harvest also. Papa thought Rex should know better and he got a bawling out but not me.

Rex grew to be a very handsome man and people often said he looked like Robert Taylor who was a heartthrob movie star of 1930s and 40s. Besides having good looks, he had a great spontaneous sense of humor and a loveable personality. Everyone liked him and he was very popular. Besides all these good things he was smart. In fact, he was valedictorian at his high school graduation. But, events during the Depression never allowed him to go to college and so he never got to live up to his potential. This bothered him most of his life while he worked as a Mill Wright in a mill on the Oregon Coast. He thought he never amounted to anything as he expressed it.

One day he said, "You know that piece of land where the two roads fork and form a triangle. I think I'll buy that whole triangle and erect a monument to myself and inscribe it with the words. 'This is a monument to Rex Lee who never amounted to anything'."

Chapter 14

Jesse was a nice gentle riding pony my sister and I could ride but we had another horse named Lightning. He earned that name because he took off like a streak of lightning the minute anyone got on his back. He was used on the farm to make a quick trip from one place to another. He helped take water to the men working in the fields or fetch tools or parts for the machinery.

We always had dogs and cats around the farm. I remember a dog named Toby but something happened to him. He might have died from a rattlesnake bite. We needed about three dogs to use as sled dogs so Papa had been looking for another dog. He didn't have to look very long because one day a mixed breed Collie showed up begging for food like a bum on the street corner. Right away Papa started calling him Bummer. Papa squirted milk at him when he was milking Old Maggie our cow and I'm pretty sure that's when Bummer decided to stay with us.

Buster was my brother's dog and Buster was always at Rex's heels. We also had Prince, a black shiny haired dog. The dogs weren't exactly pets. They had important jobs on the farm. They helped round up the horses or sometimes they hitched all three dogs to a sled to take Papa or Rex to town in winter. They warned us of snakes and kept them away. They often killed snakes. The dogs earned their keep.

I loved all the animals on our farm but Prince was special with me and I felt pretty sure he liked me better than anyone. Papa used what he called a halter chain on the horses when he wanted to tie them more securely than bridle reins did. On this particular day, I fastened one of the chains around Prince's neck to lead him around. I led Prince over by the car and he hurried to get under it to be in the shade. He was tired of playing and he wanted to lie down and rest for a while so I fastened the other end of the chain around the back bumper of the car.

"Ruthie, we are going to town. Do you want to go along or would you rather stay home with Bobel?"

"I wanta go with you."

"Hurry up then, and have Bobel get you ready to go."

I ran to the house and Mama and Papa and I were soon bumping along over the gravel road to Drummond. Papa started singing as usual and Mama and I soon joined him in an old familiar song. "Come away with me Lucille, in my merry Oldsmobile."

I felt so happy in the seat between Mama and Papa making plans about what I would ask them to buy me at the candy counter.

About half way to town we met Rex riding along the road on Lightning. When he got beside us he pulled back on the reins as hard as he could and the horse reared up with both front feet in the air. That was just Rex and Lightning's natural way of stopping suddenly. Rex had a puzzled expression on his face and he looked as if he had just seen a ghost or something.

"What's the matter with Prince?"

There was kind of a quiver in the gasping sound Rex made. When I saw him looking at the back of the car I remembered I had tied Prince to the bumper and because he was underneath the car we didn't see him when we got in the car. I realized I had forgotten to untie him when we left to go to town.

I guess he ran as long as he could behind the car and then we dragged him. He was dead.

Rex gently picked him up and placed him across the horse behind the saddle and took him home. It was a terrible scene and I was overcome with sorrow. I couldn't forgive myself for being so forgetful and causing the death of our faithful dog. I cried.

"It was an accident Ruthie, and everyone has accidents. You must try to forget about it. Maybe we can get you a puppy from Mr. Goole."

Now for the story of how Rex got Buster.

One day a man came past the farm. I met him by the gate.

"Hello little girl, I was wondering if I could get some water for me and my dog? We ran out and it's so hot today."

"Wait here and I'll find Papa and ask him if it's okay."

I found Papa in the well house where he was turning the windmill on to fill the watering troughs.

"Well, of course it's alright. Tell him to wait a minute and I'll be right there."

Papa came and gave the stooped, bearded old man the dipper that was hanging by the well. He filled the dipper with the cold water pouring from the pipe. The man looked as old as Papa did, around forty I think. Then Papa gave the dog a pan of water. Then he filled the man's canvas water bag that was hanging from the radiator cap on his car. I noticed the water bag was wet on the outside.

"Your bag is leaking no wonder you don't have any water."

"Yeah, it seeps through a little but as it evaporates it keeps the water cool inside the bag."

I didn't know what evaporates meant. I listened to them talking.

"I'm down on my luck. Things have been going from bad to worse for me. I wonder if you could help me out. I'd be willing to sell you this fine dog for five bucks. His name is Buster."

By that time, the rest of the family had gathered around, the same as they always did if someone stopped by. Rex took a liking to the brindle colored wire-haired bull terrier. Actually, he might have been what they call a pit bull. It seems to me he looked like one except he had a kind face and gentle look in his eyes a sort of pleading look.

"I got a dollar I'll give you for him!" Rex said as he reached in his pocket and brought out the silver dollar he had been saving for a pocket watch to carry in the watch pocket of his Levis.

I heard a funny chuckle the man made when he said, "Nope gotta have five dollars for this dog. He's kinda special cuz he's so smart you can teach him anything."

I felt sorry for my big brother when I saw the disappointed look on his face as he turned to walk away.

Papa was a pretty soft touch when it came to his kids.

"Wait! I'll give you the five dollars Rex. You earned it with all the help you've been lately. Guess you will soon take the place of one of the hired men around here. Anyway we could use another dog."

It was a terrible price to pay for a dog. People usually gave dogs away. People rarely give dogs away nowadays, but sell them for hundreds of dollars.

The man drove off with thick ham sandwiches Mama made for him and five silver dollars from the jar in the cupboard. As soon as he was out of sight Buster took out after him running as hard and fast as he could. He followed the man because he was his master and he loved him. The man must have been a kind master even though he turned out not to be a nice man.

Lightning was tethered on a fence post nearby. Rex jumped on him and raced after Buster. About a mile down the road he lassoed his five dollar dog with a rope and brought him back. Buster had a new master now and a whole family that loved him.

Even though he was kind to dogs, that old man was a scoundrel. We later found out the con man had sold the dog at a couple other places on his route. I guess Buster was smart all right and had been trained to run after his master, never to be found again by the buyer. Buster was a great dog and spent many years with us as a helper and companion.

Dogs and cats were never allowed in the house and Mama wouldn't even touch a cat or dog. I never understood why. Buster eventually worked his way into her heart and lived to old age in the comfort of a soft leather rocking chair where he slept day and night. Mabel took him to live on her farm after she married and there he fell in the canal and drowned.

Chapter 15

There was never a dull moment on our farm. There were interesting activities going on some place all the time. It is surprising how each day could be so different. This good fortune followed me most of my life so I never felt like I was in a rut. The farm taught me something new about life and about people every day.

I learned at a very early age to stay away from the fencerows, which was a valuable lesson that might have saved my life. It seemed the rattlesnakes like to crawl along fences. I think it was because tumbleweeds blew into the fences and it was shady there so they spent the heat of the days where it wasn't so hot to crawl on their belly. We had a long row of horseradish growing by the fence in our front yard. Papa often shot the snakes in the horseradish and the dogs kept an eye out for there for them too. After a time I guess they were all killed because I have pictures of me sitting in the horseradish.

Sometimes I watched the dogs kill snakes by shaking them hard in their mouth. When the snakes bit them, the dogs laid in the mud hole by the watering trough until they recovered from the bites.

Once we came home from town and there was a rattlesnake in the wood box behind the kitchen stove. I don't know how it got there. I remember the excitement it caused in my family. I think Mama put up with unpleasant things living on a dry farm but this incident was a bit too much.

"I want to go back home to Oregon."

I always had a warm feeling whenever I saw Papa take Mama in his arms and tell her how much he loved her. I ran over and hugged them both around their legs while Papa tried to comfort Mama.

One day Papa took me with him when he went to kill snakes. We both got on Jesse our white riding horse and with the rifle across his lap and me hanging on behind we set out. We were on our way over to Ed Goole's farm, probably to talk about harvest. Ed was an old bachelor that lived on the other side of the hill from the coyote that always watched me. People called him a hermit because he didn't socialize much. He kept to himself most of the time but he always helped with the harvest. Papa and Ed talked and laughed for a long time while I played with the new puppies.

We didn't run across any snakes on the way to Ed's so Papa decided to go home a different direction. He shot a couple of snakes and climbed down from the horse to cut the rattlers from their tails. I had a big collection of rattles I kept in a tobacco can and I played with them a lot. I liked to shake them and make them rattle to scare other kids.

By going home this direction, I realized we were going right past the coyote that watched me all summer. I knew I was safe with Papa so I really wanted to see that bad old critter close up.

As we came closer, the strangest thing happened. The coyote turned into a sagebrush. He still had the same head and ears but the rest of him didn't look anything like a coyote. From that day on I could look up on that hill and know the coyote had turned into a sagebrush. It was like magic and such a relief after I had looked for him on the hill every day and been afraid him all summer.

We often had errands in the little towns that surrounded us. Papa had a big green wagon with red wagon wheels. It was a happy occasion when Papa lifted me up on the springboard seat and took me to town with him to get supplies for the farm and house. The wagon bounced up and down over the gravel washboard road on the way to town but on the way home it rode quite smoothly it was so loaded with Papa's purchases of oats, chicken feed and other supplies.

We went past a prairie dog village in a field close to the road. They always came out of their holes to watch us go by. They stood up on their hind legs, then folded their front legs in front of them and made quick jerky movements. They seemed so curious and looked like they were chattering about the noisy wagon and the horses. They were so cute and they never took their eyes off us.

"Papa look they are watching us. Maybe they think we are cute too."

We always had different things to do and see on the farm. Even though we lived in such a remote area, there were all kinds of travelers that went past our place.

Among the more interesting travelers was a band of gypsies. They came past our farm every summer. We could hear their dogs barking and the bells on their horses echoing through our hollow long before they reached the house. Gypsies were another thing besides lightning and thunder that my Mama was terrified of and once again we hid in the bedroom. If they knocked on the door we never answered. She told me she heard they stole little children. When they were around I stayed close to the house so I could run inside if I had to.

Once Papa told the gypsies, they could camp in our big yard. They made camp and then built a fire from some of Papa's wood pile and fixed their evening meal. They played music and kind of danced around. Mama said those things they were shaking were tambourines. I peeked around the corner of the house and they seemed kind of nice to me especially the kids. I wanted to play with them but I was too afraid and too shy to venture near. The men looked a little scary but the women had pretty shawls and dresses.

I don't think they stole anything like people said they did. Anyway, they never tried to steal me but Rex's badger he had caught and penned up vanished. Still I can't imagine they wanted that mean old badger. I was scared to death of him if he even looked at me.

One thing that was lacking at the farm was other children to play with. It was good I had such a vivid imagination. The toys I played with were different than children in the towns played with. Among my homemade toys were about six stick horses that were cut from the aspen trees down by the old house. Each one had a name. Each one had reigns tied around its neck and I rode them lickity split swatting them with a willow so they went faster and when they tired I tied them by the front porch and fed them weeds.

I also had a big bag of marbles Mama made for me by rolling flour and water into little balls. She colored them with blue and red and yellow food coloring. They dried hard as rocks and they served their purpose. Later I had bag of real marbles. I think they were made of glass and had colored swirls all through them. They had names like cats eyes. There was one called a steely which looked like a ball of steel. It was my best shooter. I begged everyone to play marbles with me and kept them handy in my tobacco bag in case I got a taker. We made a big circle on the dusty ground and took turns shooting at the marbles until we got them all out of the circle. Anyway that's the way we played the game. I don't know how was supposed to be played.

I also had an old rusty wagon. I knelt one leg in the wagon and pushed myself along with the other leg guiding it by the tongue bent back. It made a good car and sometimes I tied Bummer or Prince or Buster on the tongue and made them pull me.

A good friend of the family came to the farm one day. He brought me a doll bed he made from a box.

"Ruthie, come here and see what Mr. Jacobs made for you."

I hid behind Mama's skirt not daring to go near that scary looking man until she pushed me toward him. I was a little afraid of Mr. Jacobs. He never shaved like Papa did and had a long wispy beard that blew sideways in the wind. His eyes were set back under long bushy eyebrows and his teeth were stained from chewing tobacco. I saw him pull a plug of tobacco from his pocket once and bite off a chunk. He spit some of it on the ground. It looked nasty. Some of the juice dribbled from the side of his mouth. I thought he must be a lot nicer than he looked to make such a nice a doll bed for me. Then besides the nice doll bed he handed me a candy bar which I eagerly reached for in spite of my shyness.

Mama nudged me, "What do you say to Mr. Jacobs?"

"Can I have another candy bar for my brother?"

Mama nudged me again.

"No, tell Mr. Jacobs thank you for the cute little doll bed."

My doll bed was varnished and it looked nice for many years. My sister's children inherited it from me when I decided I was too big to play with dolls any more.

Other interesting travelers on our road were the sheepherders. Every summer sheepherders drove bands of sheep past our place to take them up in the hills to eat grass. There were always little bummer lambs whose mothers had died. The lambs needed special care so they usually gave one to me. I fed them from a bottle with a long black nipple on it. I loved those little lambs and they followed me around everywhere just like 'Mary's Little Lamb'. Lambs are lots of fun and make good playmates.

I never realized Papa actually took the lambs for us to eat and until

I was older. I never knew what happened to them. I thought they just ran away. Then one day I realized from a conversation I overheard that I was eating my own little lamb's chops. I could feel my heart falling apart inside me. My heart was broken. Papa explained to me that the reason we lived on a farm and raised animals was partly for our food, but also for of the money. I understood what he was trying to tell me and I never felt such a loss when one of the animals left.

With Papa so good to explain things to me, every day was full of excitement and I loved living on the busy farm and getting to know all the people that came there.

With Jesse, the horse I loved to ride.

When the sheepherders went past our place, they always gave me a
bummer lamb.

Rex in the hired men's hat and chaps.

Rex and Papa in the certified seed potato field.

In front of the ramshackle farm house.

Governor Moore visiting the farm.

Chapter 16

We always called our parents Mama and Papa. I guess this was a family thing because my friends called their parents Mama and Daddy. Mama's mother we called Mam and Papa's mother was Mama Lee. Both grandfathers died before I was born. I never really got to know my grandmothers very well. All my relatives including my brother and sister were born in Oregon. Most of my grandparents' parents were early settlers from the east. Some came over the Oregon Trail and homesteaded land grants. One of my ancestors was mentioned in a book called Women of the Oregon Trail. He was a scoundrel horse trader and was accused of cheating people. He settled a large parcel of land around Junction City. He redeemed his horse trading days by becoming very wealthy and helping other people later settle around the Willamette Valley according to the book I read.

I was born shortly after my family moved to Idaho. My immediate family was all born in Junction City, Oregon. I was the only one ever born in Idaho.

Papa's mother outlived three husbands and all three of her children. There were a large number of relatives on Mama's side of the family, but Papa only had a brother and a sister.

Papa worked on building Highway 101 near Yachats in 1921 the summer before he moved our family to Idaho. At the time they were building the road in bits and pieces. There was no road and only a few bridges inland along the ocean so people traveled on the beach in some places while the tide was out. Other places they had to go inland and double back to get their destination. My family spent that summer in a tent near the beach while Papa worked on the road.

Mam, my mother's mother, lived at Santa Rosa when she was young, next door to Luther Burbank, an important agricultural pioneer who developed hundreds of new varieties of fruits and vegetables. Papa's mother was a relative of Carrie Nation the woman that took an axe to saloons in the early 1900s trying to close them down.

My niece traced our family genealogy back to the 1700's recently. Mama's relatives came from Switzerland, Papa's from England. Mama was thirty-two when I was born so most of the relatives had died before I was born. They died at an early age in those days.

When I was around three years old, we visited our relatives in Oregon. I remember very little about that trip except it was long and in a Model A touring car. I remember the isinglass windows we snapped on and off according to the weather. Inside the car, it was small and crowded.

I also remember Mam, my grandmother, making my cousin and me little buckets by punching holes in the top of lard cans with a nail. She put a wire through the holes to make a bale so we could carry them. We knew those cute little buckets had a useful purpose and we proceeded to find it. We went into Mam's garden and dug up most of her potato patch just keeping the tiny potatoes that fit in our little buckets. The relatives didn't like us digging up the cute potatoes and they started scolding and causing a big rumpus about the damage. Mam must have felt sorry for us.

"It's alright. They didn't mean any harm. Let's all have some of that red velvet chocolate cake shall we?"

After I was married, my husband and I moved to Oregon and we visited my grandmothers. Mam lived in Oregon City with my Aunt Thelma who owned a little diner downtown and they lived on the hill above the diner close to where an elevator lifts you to the top of the hill now.

Mam scurried about to fix my husband and me dinner. She dug little tiny potatoes out in the garden behind the house from under the vines with her fingers.

"Do you remember when you dug up my potato patch when you were little? I guess you were too little to remember that."

"Yes I do remember, but I was hoping you didn't."

It was during smelt season and Mam fried a big pan full of smelt to go with the wilted lettuce. I was used to the big trout in Idaho but smelt became a must-have for me every year when they ran in the Sandy River. I haven't seen them in the grocery stores lately. I wonder what happened to them. They were so good dipped in flour and fried in bacon grease to a crispy golden brown served with buttery little new potatoes with the skins on just as Mam fixed them the day we visited.

Mama Lee lived in Junction City. She was so excited to see her granddaughter when my husband and I visited her that she grabbed me and gave me a big crushing bear hug. She smelled of tobacco smoke. We settled down in old antique rocking chairs among dozens of other antiques to chat. That's when she pulled out a corn cob pipe gave it a few knocks against a dish she used for an ash tray and filled the bowl of the pipe with tobacco she pressed into it with her thumb. It didn't hold much because it was so full of ugly brown crud from previous half burned tobacco stuck to the sides. She took a couple puffs on the pipe and then laid the pipe in the dish.

"Hope you didn't mind my smoke. You don't have this nasty habit do you? Come with me I want you to see my new bed."

We were scared to tell her we both smoked.

She pulled off the new sheets and blankets to show us the blue mattress and pointed to little round circles on the sides of the mattress with screens over them.

"I guess they put these holes in the mattress to let the farts out."

Both my husband and I stood there aghast and then started laughing uncontrollably. Grandmothers just never talked in such an undignified manner!

She opened an old round top trunk and on the very top of a lifetime of keepsakes was the clothing she planned for her burial clothes. She took out each item and showed them to us including a white dress, pearls, undies, white shoes and silk stockings.

A few years later, she decided she wanted to visit her family in Idaho and since she didn't have much money and her family thought at eighty she was too old to travel she decided to hitchhike and that's just what she did. I wish I knew the details of her last trip. She died in Idaho. I hope she had the clothes from her trunk.

My grandmother was what people call a 'character' and I'm pretty sure my sister and I both inherited a bit of this tendency from her. In fact, not too long ago someone told me I was a character.

Chapter 17

Each summer we packed up the car with blankets, food, pans and all the camping gear. There was an expandable metal luggage rack that attached to the running boards of the car so the running boards could be used to carry a few of the supplies. Papa built a cupboard like box on the back of the car to hold camping gear. Once the car was loaded, we headed over the mountains to explore Yellowstone Park.

Our farm was located just a few miles away from the western side of the Grand Tetons across from Jackson Hole, Wyoming. Across the rolling hills of our farm and from the house we had in Ashton we always had a breathtaking view of those majestic mountains.

The Teton Pass in the twenties was very steep. Modern road building has made it less so. I wonder if the old Model T's and Model A's were equipped with brakes that could handle such steep mountain passes. I remember seeing little trees tied to the back of cars in an attempt to slow them down as they descended the mountain pass.

The Frenches and Aunt Ed's family went with us when we camped in Yellowstone. Their cars were loaded too with everything from big sides of bacon to honey for the campfire biscuits. Just what bears like to eat. Everything was stored in big metal cans and tall milk cans and we could hear bears and other wild animals wandering through our camp at night.

People left the bears alone and did not feed or agitate them or encourage them to visit. The animals never seemed to bother us as we kept a clean camp and a distance. There were so many bears then but later they were removed from certain areas of the Park to protect people from their own foolishness and to protect the bears from the bad habits they acquired from being around humans. I don't know if the removed bears ever returned to the park.

In those days, people were naturally careful to keep that great area the gorgeous place it was. Of course, not so many people visited as now. We drove right up to the geysers and explored every place. Now, many of the sights we saw are 'closed to the public'. Some of the pools and geysers have changed, moved or are gone altogether. An earthquake several years ago changed many of the sights.

When I was small I heard someone talking about a lady that backed her car into the Morning Glory Pool and disappeared forever. I always wondered if this was true so I asked a ranger about it when I went to Yellowstone a few years ago.

"Funny you should ask. I read something about it a couple days ago and yes it is true."

We didn't use a tent when we camped. We stretched a canvas tarp from the top of the car and staked the bottom of it away from the car forming a sort of lean-to. The whole family crawled under there together beneath the heavy wool crazy quilts. What fun we had talking half the night. Mama and Papa were so happy to be among the trees. They missed the big forests of Oregon.

By taking several bus tours, I've been fortunate enough to have traveled in all but two of the United States and all the provinces of Canada. I've seen most of their most attractive sights and beauty. While a lot of them may be equal to the Grand Tetons, nothing surpasses them and their grandeur and nothing is more unusual and breathtaking than Yellowstone Park. What a great place to have spent my happy early years. I'm sure that it gave me my overwhelming appreciation of the great outdoors and all the splendor of God's Creation. I'm filled with heartfelt gratitude that I've had this tremendous opportunity to travel around the United States during my lifetime.

The second great annual event of my childhood west of the Tetons was the sled dog races held in Ashton in February every year. There were many dog teams in the local area. A great number came from other states and even other countries. Ashton became the best known town in the world in those days because of all the publicity and more than 10,000 attended the races. It was a two or three day affair as I remember. The dogs raced around a long track that was especially prepared around the town of Ashton. Such beautiful dogs, mostly huskies, but all breeds that liked to run. They worshipped their masters and were anxious to please them. The kids had their races around a shorter track. They still have these dog races and I wish I could go and see them once again. I haven't been to the dog races in Ashton since I left there when I was eleven.

It was such fun with my friends during the days of the races. We roamed the streets among the crowds in and out of the hotels and restaurants where grown-ups were dancing and drinking. These were the days of the "flappers" and some of the women had taken up smoking and drinking. You might say the whole town was whooping it up.

I got a shiny new sled from Santa one year. A mean boy took it away from me and I never got it back. I showed an older brother of his my name on the bottom of the sled but he just laughed and walked away. Several years after that I saw him participating in the dog races in Truckee, California.

Chapter 18

After we moved into Ashton to spend the stormy winters away from the farm I had friends to play with for the first time. When their fathers heard about the big fish in the Teton River behind our house at the farm the men were anxious to go fishing as soon as winter was over. After that, we often had company and I showed the kids all the wonders of living on a farm.

We made a playhouse by hanging the old army blankets from World War I on the clothesline. We made mud pies from water and dirt and birds eggs we robbed from the pigeon's nests on top of the granary. We had a large flock of pigeons. They made a cooing sound unlike any bird I ever heard as they strutted across the roof of the granary. Papa often shot sage hens or pheasants that we ate but we never ate the pigeons. It seems I remember that some people did eat them.

My friends and I found old spice cans from the garbage dump behind the barn and filled them with dirt, which we sprinkled on our various mud dishes we baked in the sun. We had orange crates that made great cupboards to store our assortment of cookware made up of tin cans and old discarded pans that had the enamel chipped off and chipped dishes and plates Mama had thrown away.

In my high school yearbook one of my fellow classmates wrote, "Never forget the mud pies we used to make." As you can see I have never forgotten very many things about that time in my life.

No, I never have forgotten Phyllis either but when I think of her I remember a sad time. Her sister was lying on her stomach drinking water from a stream on her father's farm. Her teenage brother who was looking at a rifle accidentally dropped it and it fired. The bullet hit her and she died. Though I came from a family of hunters from that day to this day I've never been able to stand the sight of a gun or the thought of killing anything or anybody with a gun.

My sister on the other hand was an avid hunter and every hunting season she filled her quota of game. One time when she was over eighty, they had to bring her out of the woods in an ambulance. She never went the year she was ninety and around Christmas of that year she went on to the Great Hunting Grounds above.

The kids always liked Jesse when they came to the farm to visit. Most of them had never ridden a horse and my friend Mary fell in love with Jesse and kept asking me if she could ride her. I had been told that children were never to ride the horses and I couldn't ride either unless a grown up went with me.

"Just let me sit on her and you lead her around." Mary insisted.

Jesse had a bridle on and was standing by a fence with the bridle tied to a fence post. I thought it wouldn't hurt for Mary to sit on her a little while. Before I knew it we were both on Jesse's bare back and headed out on the road and up the hill toward the mail box.

Jesse plodded along like the nice gentle horse she was, often glancing curiously over her shoulder at the young riders on her back giggling and having a great time.

Jesse had one ornery streak and that was the reason my folks didn't want kids to ride her alone. When she took a notion to have her own way she did a kind of side step that could throw the rider off her back and land them slick as a whistle in a heap on the ground.

After we had ridden a short distance, Mary got very excited. "Make her run!"

Jesse didn't pay any attention when we tried to make her run by kicking her in the sides. She just never liked to run and she kept plodding along in her own stubborn way. That is until we decided to turn around and go home. Just one kick in the sides and Jesse started running as fast as her legs would go in long leaping strides.

Mary was in the back hanging on to me and pulling me every which way. I hung on to Jesse's mane and dug my heels into her belly. We bounced around and up and down and sideways but managed to stay on all the way home. We were lucky Jesse never took a notion to do her sneaky side step and throw us off.

All four of our parents plus my brother and sister lined up in a row across the road in front of the house. I'll never forget the look on their faces. It was pitiful. Guess I've forgotten what happened next.

I had playmates in Ashton and it was hard to move back to the farm in spring and leave them. I hated to leave the farm and move back to town in the winter too.

In town, we raked the leaves in the fall and had neighborhood bonfires. The neighbors gathered to sing, roast spuds, tell spooky stories or just sit around the fire and talk. People's faces glowed when the fire light bounced around and made them look scary so I stayed close to Mama while they told frightening stories.

Halloween was not the same as kids know it nowadays. I never heard of trick or treat until the forties. Big kids just did the tricks, which were pretty awful sometimes. There were people that still had outdoor privies in Ashton. Of course, kids tipped most of them over on Halloween. One time big boys put a car on top of the school. They soaped or waxed windows, which was very hard to get off. They saved up rotten eggs for throwing. Mostly, Halloween, especially for the little kids, took place in churches where witches met us at the door and nearly scared us to death. They dressed all in black and ran around on brooms. Their faces were white with flour and sooty black splotches. With deep gravelly spooky voices they poked their fingers at us and warned us, "The goblins are gonna getcha if you don't watch out."

We had smelly little masks to wear that got all wet around the nose and mouth and kind of melted in the wet spots. I can't imagine what they were made of. I don't remember seeing any fancy costumes but there were lots of ghosts in sheets or funny items and clothes they found around the house.

We drank apple cider or cocoa and ate homemade doughnuts or cookies decorated with black cats and ghosts. There was candy that looked like corn or pumpkins. We carried a pumpkin made into a Jack-O-Lantern with a candle that most of the mothers wouldn't let us light for fear we might burn the church down. Now that I'm old I don't like Halloween but when I was little I think I liked being scared by make believe ghosts and goblins.

We didn't attend church too often but we always went to church on Christmas Eve and Santa came bursting in the back door carrying a big bag over his shoulder. He ran around the room laughing a kind of silly Ho Ho Ho and handing every child a red felt stocking filled with chocolate drops and curly hard candy all stuck together. In the toe of the stocking, there was always a nice big orange. I noticed something about his white beard that reminded me of the cotton Mama put in her quilts when she made them. I puzzled over that beard for a long time.

"Ho! Ho! Ho! Little girl have you been good or bad?"

It was enough to scare you half out of your wits.

"I've been good Santa Clause. Bring me a pair of black patent leather shoes."

Papa went the day before Christmas and cut a Christmas tree and that night we strung popcorn and cranberries into garlands and decorated the tree with them. Mama got a box of ornaments from the storeroom, mostly little birds that clamped on the branches and some little candles too. She had little candle holders she clipped to the tree branches. She put the little twisted candles with yellow, red and blue stripes in the holders. Mama lit the candles but only briefly, because she thought they might catch the tree on fire. I think those same candles lasted all through my childhood.

Papa killed the mean old goose that chased me and bit at my legs every time I got near him. We ate him for Christmas dinner. Mama said he was a little tough. I thought he was good. After dinner, Rex rubbed goose grease all over the new skis he got for Christmas.

In the winter all my friends in Ashton played after dark in the snow under the ark light. We called streetlights ark lights. We would lie on our backs spread our legs and arms out and move them up and down making snow angels. We had snowball fights, shouted and screamed until people hollered, "Shut up and go to bed!"

Ten or twelve kids played baseball or hopscotch or kick the can or jump rope. We had a long rope held between two people and three or four children would jump at once. Sometimes there were two ropes held in each hand and turned in opposite directions. This went on for hours each evening. What good cheap entertainment we had. Mama said she could always count eight to ten children on our big front porch or in the yard. Kids loved my Mama. Who else would have had a gang like that around all the time? She always passed out some of her taffy or fudge or sugar cookies. I can still feel how proud I felt to have my mother when I remember those good times she shared with so many.

Chapter 19

The house in Ashton was more modern than our house on the farm. We even had a telephone with a crank that hung on the wall but it wasn't connected to the telephone company. Rex told me it would only work to call Bronc Sparkman the sheriff if I was naughty. All they had to do was look up at the phone if I even thought of acting up and it scared me into good behavior for the whole day. As it turned out Bronc Sparkman, who dressed more like a cowboy than a sheriff, became a good friend to me and I wasn't a bit scared of him anymore.

As I think about the house in Ashton memories flood my mind some pleasant and some not. I thought our new house in town was so nice. It even had indoor plumbing and there were electric lights hanging from the ceiling only I couldn't reach the chain to pull them on. Mama tied a string on it and ran it over to the wall so it wouldn't hang in the way and I could reach it.

The bathroom was much larger than most and had a trap door down into the cellar where Mama's home canned fruit and vegetables and potatoes and squash and other vegetables were stored. We went down around Twin Falls every fall and got several kinds of apples. My favorites were the little crab apples and wine saps. Oh, and I must not forget the big crock of sauerkraut sitting in the corner of the cellar with a big round rock on a plate on top to weigh it down as it fermented. I loved sauerkraut right out of the crock icy cold and deliciously juicy. We ate sauerkraut fixed lots of delicious ways but especially with pork chops.

Every time Mama cooked our meals it seemed she had to go down in the cellar to get something. The trap door leaned against the wall but it stood almost straight up. There was a hook to hold it up but one day the door fell on Mama's head.

"Ruthie, come here and help me."

"Oky dok in a minute."

I went ahead playing with the checkerboard and it was a long time before I answered her call. I couldn't see her any place so I knew she must be in the cellar, but why was the door down? I lifted up the trap door. The door was so heavy I could hardly move it. She was lying on the steps. She had held the door as long as she could until she finally collapsed. She got up but was in kind of a daze. I started crying and ran to get the neighbors.

Mama had terrific headaches the rest of her life. I still have a guilty conscience for not coming when she called me. After that, I always came immediately when she called.

There was something else about that extra-large bathroom. It was a lean-to addition on the house. It had a secret door. The door looked just like the wall and you wouldn't notice it was even there. Papa was surprised when he found it. The door opened into a very small room.

I heard Papa say, "You know I bet that room was used to hide something. Maybe it was illegal gambling games of poker or bootleg whiskey."

We had it piled full of junk like empty fruit jars so you could hardly get in it.

This was during prohibition when selling booze was illegal. I think my Papa might have become a bootlegger soon after that. What makes me think that is that the bathroom floor was covered with around fifteen or so gallon jugs full of a liquid that looked just like whisky now that I think about it. I didn't know what it was at the time. They yelled at me when I lifted the blanket to peek. Times were hard and money became hard to get. People did what they could to live. People that drank had to lift their spirits just the same as they they do nowadays I guess.

During winter, Papa drove a team of horses to our house in town taking a shortcut across the fields and over the tops of the fences because of the depth of the snow. He could only stay overnight with us because the livestock needed to be cared for at the farm. Mama used to stand at the kitchen window and watch for him when it was about time for him to come back from the farm. We ran to meet him when he got to yon end of the big field behind our house. He reached down to swing Mama up in the sleigh beside him. I was next. The reunion seemed as though he had been gone for months instead of only two or three days.

Papa kept the horses in a barn behind the house in town. There was a pigpen beside the barn. It hadn't been used for years so there was no evidence it had housed pigs. The pen was about a foot taller than me in the tallest part and sloped down in the back. Grown-ups couldn't stand up in it. In front, it had a wall tall enough to keep pigs in and was open the rest of the way up. Papa thought it looked like a good playhouse so he set about fixing it up for me.

He piled sawdust all over the dirt floor and made table and chairs and orange crate cupboards. He made walls all the way up. I loved it and so did my friends.

One day in the playhouse, I talked my friend Erma into having a milkweed sawdust cigarette with me. I guess I had always enjoyed watching the hired men smoking and blowing smoke rings.

The milkweed grew nearby and when it dries up it has a hollow stem so we picked some and filled it with sawdust from the floor of the pigpen. Take my word for it this makes the most rotten tasting hottest cigarette you can ever imagine. We sputtered and coughed but it wouldn't go away. My tongue felt burned and my throat was even worse. Much more of that and we would have been sick. The smell alone was enough to make us choke and throw up.

Erma ran home as fast as she could go. I think she got sick. I hurried to get rid of our cigarette evidence in case Mama showed up. She did show up, ducked her head under the low door, and looked in. The first thing she saw was the box of matches in my cupboard.

"What are you doing with that box of matches in here?"

I knew Mama thought lying was the worst sin anyone could commit so I told her the truth. I wasn't allowed in the playhouse for a month and by that time a snow-bank almost covered it over.

A neighbor boy used to come to our house a lot. He could cook up the best ideas for things to build in the snow. He was always the boss. This time it was going to be a tunnel through the big snowdrift between his house and ours. He would start on the side by his house and me on my side and we would meet in the middle. I didn't think I would like the job and told him so but he told me to get to work.

I dug into the snow bank maybe two feet. It was cold and I decided to go in the house and get warm. I sat by the warm stove and played with a deck of cards. I didn't go back out to my job digging my side of the tunnel. I heard a loud pounding on the door. When I opened the door, Teddy stood there looking pretty mad.

"What are you doing in here? You're supposed to be digging your side of the tunnel."

Mama heard the word tunnel. "Tunnel, what tunnel? Don't go digging any tunnels. You'll be buried alive. You go on home now Teddy. Ruthie isn't going out any more today."

Boy was I happy not to be going outside any more today!

Chapter 20

I lacked about three months of being six when my folks caught me, tied a pair of shoes on me and sent me to school. After going barefoot all summer, it was quite a shock. I wasn't sure I wanted to go but everyone had been telling me how great it was and that I could learn to read. I wanted to read books all by myself.

What really bothered me were those shoes with laces and the funny looking long ribbed stockings Mama ordered from Montgomery Ward's Catalog. Most people called that department store Monkey Ward or Wards and it was very popular because of the reasonable prices. Wards went out of business a few years ago so I suppose there are people that haven't heard of what used to be an important part of the American way of life.

Thinking of that important day in my life makes my heart speed up a little just as it did that morning when I thought about my three new store bought dresses. My clothes were always homemade by Mama or Mabel on the treadle sewing machine. Some were made from sacks the flour came in. Sometimes the sacks had pretty little flowers or figures all over them. They even made my bloomers to match. Talk about recycling, Mama was way ahead of the times.

My new brown oxfords were one big disappointment after I had seen the shiny patent leather baby doll shoes in the catalog that buttoned with a glass button on the side. Mama thought the oxfords were more practical and she got them too big because she thought I was growing so fast I would soon grow into them. It was a nice fall day and too early for long hot socks anyway even if they were brand new.

"Come on Ruthie, you don't want to be late on your first day of school. Here let me pull your socks up. They have wrinkled down around your ankles. These shoes are a little big but you will grow into them."

"Hurry, Hurry, Hurry. Doug's here in his new roadster to take you and Rex to school. You look so grown up in that dress. It is so cute with the puffed sleeves. I really like your hair cut short with bangs. Now don't let them stick you in that rumble seat! If Doug hits a hole in the road you'll bounce out."

Mama worried about everything. She probably visualized me lying along the road and them not even knowing they lost me.

She hugged me tightly and her face felt wet against mine. I think she hated to see the baby grow up. She wished I could stay little and be home with her. Mabel and Rex would soon be grown and leaving the nest.

Ashton was about twelve miles away over a rough washboard dirt road that wandered over hilly dry farm land. Those old 1920 cars bumped up and down every chance they got.

The wheat in the fields along the road was harvested, but the stubble was still standing. It was kind of a golden color. Soon the farmers would summer fallow the stubble under and prepare the ground for spring wheat. The fields looked naked without the heads of bearded grain blowing in the breeze. The air with a smell of grain and warm dry earth filled my nose and made me sneeze as usual.

Standing in the field in some places were bundles of straw, tied with binding twine waiting to be loaded on the wagon and hauled to the barn to be used for bedding for animals or other things that straw was needed for.

What a wonderful day to be starting school and to feel so grown up sitting between my big brother Rex and Doug his best friend who I adored. I don't remember my proposal to Doug but it was rumored that I asked him to wait for me to grow up so we could get married. I got teased about this even after I was grown and he was married to a woman with two children from a former marriage. Except for the long socks this first day on my way to school was a day beyond my wildest dreams.

That is until we ran into the red razor back pig. I don't know where he came from but suddenly there was a roly poly pig in the middle of the road just as we came over the top of the hill. I heard a loud thud and the bump threw me forward. Next thing I saw was that big fat hog rolling down the hill. He stopped rolling shortly and stood up. He looked back over his shoulder at the car and grunted insults at us then slowly walked away. Rex and Doug thought it was funny. I didn't. Poor pig.

I'm not sure why they couldn't drive the car after we hit the pig but I think the fender or bumper bent against the tire and they couldn't pull it away.

"We gotta get to school early for football practice. What're we gonna do?"

"Let's send Ruthie back to Fred's and he can take her home. Then Papa can come and pull the car home. We can walk the rest of the way to school. If we hurry, we can still make it in time for football practice. I hope we don't have to pay that farmer anything for hitting his pig."

I don't remember much after that except how scary it was along that road all alone. I remember running and crying even though no one could hear me. I kept watching for snakes by the fence and coyotes in the fields. I even thought I heard a snake hissing.

The new shoes were rubbing blisters but I couldn't go barefoot because of the puncture weed that grew near the road. I might get another of those stickers in my foot and I knew how much that hurt.

I can sure remember when Rex finally came home and the bawling out he got for leaving me alone on the road. I'll tell you what. It did me good to hear it.

Because of that pig, I missed my first day of school but Papa fixed the car and we went back early the next morning. It was the start of my second first day in school and it turned out even worse than running into a pig on that first day of my first day of school.

"There's a little girl in my room that says she lives in Hog Holler. Where is Hog Holler anyway? I never heard of it."

"Me neither."

Rex was waiting in the hall to speak to the Principal. He overheard the conversation between the first grade teacher and the Principal. He knew they were talking about me. He stepped into the room.

"Excuse me. That must be my little sister. My Dad raises hogs in the hollow where our farm is and the neighbors started calling the road past our place Hog Hollow so she thinks that's our address. " Rex gave them the correct address but I can't remember it now.

"Oh yes. I see here on her papers she won't be six until November

30th. Is that right?"

"Yes Sir."

"Well if that's the case she can't start school until next year. She isn't old enough."

"Oh no, she is going to be so disappointed."

"Can't help it. Rules are rules."

Rex never told me until we got home that day that I couldn't start school for another year. The first thing I did was take those big shoes off so Mama could look at my blisters. The hugs and kisses eased the pain of the blisters but I suffered that painful disappointment every time I thought about how long a year is.

The next fall I rode with Rex and Doug to my third first day of school. I would soon be seven and the advantage of being older made me smarter than most of the other kids. Mabel had taught me a lot in that year too.

Chapter 21

One of the highlights of our days on the farm was getting the mail. Our mailbox was about a mile from the house. Seems no one really wanted to go get it because it was so far. Often Mama and I walked to get the mail. Usually it was only the paper.

If one of the riding horses, Jesse or Lightning was available, it was a quick trip for Rex or Papa. Papa hurriedly grabbed the newspaper to read what Will Rogers had to say and he read it aloud to us. I didn't understand what it meant but I enjoyed their comments and chuckles and the way they seemed to enjoy it.

Papa and Mama were always interested in the paper as soon as we got it but they took time to enjoy the comics with me. Blondie and Dagwood, Mutt and Jeff, Little Orphan Annie, Maggie and Jiggs appeared in the comic section. Jiggs just loved corned beef and cabbage. There were also paper dolls to cut out and I had a pretty metal candy box that Mama got for Mother's day filled with paper dolls and paper dresses for each paper doll.

They talked about what was in the paper that day. Most of the stories were about President Hoover, or the price of wheat or what the politicians were going to do about the Depression. They discussed politics a lot because Papa was a Republican and Mama was a Democrat. They always made sure they voted and then laughed about canceling out the others vote.

Election Day was an important day and a time for celebration and we could always celebrate because either Papa or Mama was happy their side won. Crowds of people spent the day in St. Anthony waiting for the returns of the election to come in.

When we drove up to the voting place there were already several Model T. Fords parked there. Tied at the hitching post were horses with wagons. Kids were running everywhere. I'm not sure if we were at a schoolhouse or a grange hall or church. It all seemed exciting to me. I saw one man waving his arms and shaking his finger in another man's face.

"We gotta get that guy out of there and get someone else with common sense."

I don't know who he was talking about. He said something about a chicken in every pot and about somebody running. Everything was confusing to me.

A man stood by a blackboard and wrote down numbers as the results of the election came in to him. I guess he got the results over the phone. Some people cheered when their candidate was ahead. Others slumped down and looked glum.

Women ran around serving snacks and coffee. Men went outside and smoked. They drank from a flat shaped bottle they passed around. Kids played games but mostly we just ran around screaming and having fun. Election Day was one important event that everybody went to.

I guess my parents made me become half Democrat and half Republican as there are things about each party I detest and things about each party I admire. Does that make me a Republucrat?

I'm positive the reason I'm able to recall my early childhood so vividly was due to our family discussions every day. We talked about what happened to each of us during the day and to the neighbors.

Through the papers we knew what was going on in the world. The Denver Post and the Ashton Herald were our main sources of information. I seem to remember the Saturday Evening Post and another magazine we got in the mail along with the Farmer's Almanac that came once a year. Mama planted everything when it was time to plant according to the signs in the almanac. I think of my parents as very well informed in spite of the remote area where we lived and I think they were very intelligent though not educated beyond High School.

The conversations permanently impressed on my mind the wonderful and sometimes sad memories I carry with me. I have memories from the time when I was only two which I've been told makes me a unique person. Not very many people have this ability. I proved it by answering questions about places and things I couldn't have known unless I had actually seen or heard them. For instance a house I described to my mother perfectly in later years that burned down when I was a little over two years old and I can still see the inside of it.

To this day, I recall an incident that happened in that house when my cousin Harold came to visit. I see us in a bedroom with dark green wallpaper and even darker green woodwork. It is daytime but the dull light bulb hanging from the ceiling is on because the whole house has such dark paint it always seems dark everywhere.

I have a baby doll that looks like a real baby and Harold grabs it from me. Teasing me, he puts it against the swinging mirror on the dresser so I can't reach it. It falls through the swinging mirror and down behind the dresser. I start screaming. Maybe Harold thinks Mama will come running when she hears me. He hurries to get the doll from behind the dresser and shoves her in my hands. Her head is spilt open. I'm stomping my feet and screaming to high heaven even louder than before. Mama comes running in the room. Harold runs outside. That's all I can remember.

In the world today we are so interested in TV and the movies and acquiring the material advantages available to us that we neglect learning others' thoughts and feelings. Each day just blends into the next without printing them in our minds. It almost seems like a free for all with everyone putting self-interest ahead of anything else. An attitude of I got mine but I don't care if anybody else gets theirs.

From now on some of the stories of my life are sad stories but that was my life through no fault of my own or anyone else's. I've been lucky to have loved and been loved by good, kind and decent people. I always received the love and respect from my husband and my children and my one and only grandchild. I'm very grateful for my childhood memories of my parents. What more could I ask for. I count my blessings.

Chapter 22

During the harvest of the year that I was eight, Rex caught his arm in the belt of the combine. It lifted him off his feet and he was hanging by his arm which was twisted between the belt and the wheel it turned on. Papa ran a great distance to the house to get the car to take Rex to the doctor. Rex recovered, but with some permanent damage to his arm. It was weaker for the rest of his life because of the pulled ligaments. I wonder if the stress of that day had anything to do with Papa's illness soon after that.

Not long after Rex's accident Papa became very ill with acute nephritis. The doctors called it Bright's disease. After six weeks in the Spencer Hospital in Idaho Falls, on Rex's eighteenth birthday October 29, 1931, Papa died. He was forty-two years old. Mama was forty and I was eight. He was born December 23, 1887. My life would never be the same again and it was the first of the many times that events in my life changed my way of life completely.

I adored and admired my father and so did everyone that knew him. He was such a happy man enjoying life to the fullest with his sense of humor, his ability to show his love and his kindness to other people. He was always there to help. His great example of responsibility and his set of values made every life he touched better. My Papa was a good, kind, gentle, honest man. He was a wise man and I thought he knew everything. I have such wonderful memories of my first eight years of life that I spent with my family. We were a very close family because family came first with my parents.

I didn't cry. I don't think I felt how final death is for the ones left behind. It didn't seem real. I watched my family struggling with sorrow and grief at his funeral. I couldn't understand. One red rose was pinned above his head and as they closed the lid of his casket, it finally came to me that I wouldn't see him again. I had a feeling same as I had when he told me goodnight every night. It was as though he had just said to me, "Goodnight, my little Angel."

It became very clear to me later that Papa was missing and our family had fallen apart. He wouldn't be there to kiss my hurts or give me a penny for an all-day sucker. We would never catch grasshoppers together so we could go fishing. Nor would he help me up on old Jesse to go hunting for sage hens. I would never help him pull the pretty feathers from the ducks he shot by the lake. Who would dance with me at the Warm River dances?

Old Bummer, who had followed every footstep Papa took, stayed by the gate and watched for Papa to come home. He eventually refused to eat and got so weak he died. Mama thought he grieved himself to death. How great can a dog's love be?

Rex graduated from high school the following spring. His chances of college were gone. Still a teenager he tried to take Papa's place for a while until our lives changed even more. Things were never the same again.

I remember the day God took you away.
It's as though it was only yesterday.
Just a child I was only eight.
But the legacy you left I appreciate.

Each Father's Day I celebrate what I had.
My father the world's greatest Dad.
Decades pass but you live on in my mind.
Precious are my memories of a perfect time.

I see you now a lank and tall six foot three.
Jolly mirth filled eyes as blue as they can be.
Callused hands thinning hair and captivating grin.
That Kirk Douglas cleft in the middle of your chin.

I hear your old time songs on the way to town.
In our Model T Ford always bouncing around.
On washboard roads over rocks and fills.
Your vibrant voice echoing through rolling hills.

Winters going for rides in a covered sleigh.
While bells on harness jingled all the way.
I rode around fields with you on a drill or a plow.
Or I trod along beside you to bring in the cow.

Summers and grasshoppers we put on a hook.
Fishing for trout in a Rocky Mountain brook.
Glorious camping trips in Yellowstone Park.
Listening to animals' scary sounds after dark.

You let me pull my own tooth you tied on a string.
Then kissed away the tears a lost tooth can bring.
My daily chores with you were more like play.
Feeding chickens, gathering eggs at close of day.

You whittled, carved or built my toys.
Though more like toys for little boys.
A tall swing a willow whittled into a whistle.
Clothespin rubber band a board made into a pistol.

You told me things I needed to know.
How to tie my shoes what made stars glow.
You taught me to ride a pony and use a curry comb.
To care for baby chicks in their chicken coop home.

I learned to be good by the example you set.
Your love for life and family remain with me yet.
Thank you for teaching me to love nature.
Our great outdoors, and every living creature.

These memories are but a few.
Of the many stored in my heart of you.
Thanks for all the love and fun we had.
My wonderfully delightful, dearest Dad.

Chapter 23

Mama, Rex and I spent that winter after Papa died in a neighbor's original two-room log house where they lived before they built a new house. It was close to our farm so Rex could take care of the animals.

Rex put on snowshoes and walked over the snow to the farm about a mile and a half from the house we were staying in. The snow drifted so high that his journey was impassable that winter any other way than snowshoes or skis. Snowshoes were a wide gut webbed contraption that you slid your overshoes into and you could walk on top of the snow. They were about two and a half feet long and a foot and a half wide narrowing down to a point at the back.

Rex proved he was a reliable and responsible teenager as he took on the duties of a farmer's son during that cold miserable winter when bad spells of weather plagued our life.

Rex got a job driving our team of horses and sleigh picking up children along the route to school in Drummond, the closest town to our farm. We had a little pot-bellied stove in the canvas topped sleigh and lots of Mama's heavy wool quilts. The floor was covered with straw and blankets. We were cozy on the seven-mile trip.

One day it was forty below zero and they couldn't heat the school so they sent us back home in the bitter cold. The horses had long icicles hanging from their faces and frost on their backs from their heavy breathing drifting back across their bodies. They bent their heads down and struggled to pull the load under these conditions. The snow under their feet made crisp crackly sounds as their hooves struck the hard icy road. My brother had us get out and run a little to keep our blood circulating faster and to keep us from freezing. We had scarves over our faces so as not to breathe the frozen air into our lungs. We finally got back to the little log cabin and to Mama's warm fire and hot mulligan stew. She told us we had to stay home the next time the thermometer dipped below zero.

That winter I had terrible earaches and ear infections. The teacher made a bed for me with coats on the little chairs and tried to comfort me. These infections have plagued me all my life so now I'm left with very little hearing.

Along with the onion poultices Mama put on me at the first sign of a cold and the liniment she doctored other ailments with she had a cure for earaches too. She used warm drops of sweet oil held in my ears with cotton. Even worse was the times she had someone blow cigarette smoke in my ears. I'm not sure what it was supposed to do but whatever it was it didn't do it as I remember.

There are three memories that stand out in my mind of Drummond school days. The best thing is that I learned to love poetry from the teacher I had that year. She had us memorizing a new poem at least once a month and I still remember some of them. Writing poetry is now my favorite pastime.

Another thing I remember was that I finally got old enough to use the hole in my desk that held a bottle of ink. I finally got a pen that I dipped in the bottle of ink to write. Later fountain pens came into use. I read recently that they invented ballpoint pens 75 years ago. It seems only yesterday when I learned to do push and pulls in penmanship class with the pen I dipped in ink and where we learned the Palmer Method style of penmanship.

Something happened at Drummond that I never got completely over. I became the victim of a group of girl bullies. I grew to hate and dread going to school and I had always loved school before. What made them want to torment me I'll never know. Maybe it was because of my shyness that they could get away with it. I was so scared of them that I was afraid to tell anyone even Mama for fear of what the bullies would do to me if I ever told. Besides one the worst things a kid could do was be a tattletale.

Finally, one day when they were following me upstairs jabbing at my legs and laughing I couldn't take it any longer. I made a fist and quickly turned and socked the leader as hard as any adult could have right in her open jaw. She must have bit her tongue and it started bleeding.

That is just when my teacher showed up. I felt like running. I didn't want her to think I was bad. She must have known what was going on so without saying a word, she marched the girls to the principal's office and left me standing there. The girls were nice to me after that. Drummond school wasn't so bad after all. To this day when I hear of bullying in schools I feel the terror of it. What makes a bully a bully I wonder?

Chapter 24

Mama never went back to the farm after that hard winter. When Papa went to the hospital, someone stole the harvested sacks of wheat out of the fields. With the wheat stolen we had no income that year.

I don't why Mama ever let Rex take Papa's $500 insurance money and buy a new car. On the way to see his girlfriend in St. Anthony he totaled the new car with only a few miles on it and that was the end of the insurance money and the car.

In the spring, the house burned down. There was nothing left in the ashes of the Monarch range, the potbellied stove, the treadle sewing machine or any other metal. There was strong evidence that someone stole all the furnishings and then set fire to the house.

Mama and I went back to the house we owned in Ashton and Rex went to live with Doug's folks. He worked for them for room and board. Our families had been friends since their days in Oregon and Rex became part of their family. Mama lost the dry farm.

Mama rented out the two front rooms of our house in Ashton and the two of us lived in the back part of the house. The renters had to come through our part of the house to use the bathroom and to get water so there wasn't much privacy for either family. We managed to live on the rent money, which I think was about ten dollars a month. My sister helped us as much as she could.

Mama worked for a while in the fall in the seed house for eight dollars a week. The seed house was where they sorted bad dried seed peas from the good seed peas by hand picking them off a belt that came along in front of the women sitting on stools on each side. Later she got a job in the creamery, which was much better.

I was home alone until Mama got off work at nine. I wanted to do things to help her and so I would think of things to surprise her with like mopping the floor or cleaning the bathroom. The praise she heaped on me was well worth the work. I knew I had the best Mama on earth.

There was one thing I always did that I didn't dare let her know about. I loved to chop the kindling she used to start the fire with in the morning but she always told me not to use the ax. Ever.

"You are too little to be chopping wood. Remember that time the ax slipped and went right through Papa's shoe and cut his big toe?"

One day I heard her telling someone, "I've got the best neighbors. Every night they cut kindling for me and stack it on the porch."

I was afraid she would faint if I told her I chopped the kindling so I never told her until after I was grown and I thought she was going to faint then.

She did something almost as dangerous as chopping wood. She propped one end of the stick of kindling against the stove and the other end on her chest and made shavings right on the stick by pulling a sharp butcher knife up toward her.

She scratched a match on the matchbox and set fire to the shavings. Then she laid these shaving sticks under little pieces of coal to get the coal to start burning. Sometimes if she couldn't get the fire started she poured kerosene on the kindling.

Often in the morning, the teakettle sitting on the stove had ice in it from the freezing temperatures through the night. We stoked the heating stove full of coal before we went to bed but sometimes the coal wouldn't last all night and the temperature dropped fast when it got below zero.

I wonder how many times I've heard people say, "We were poor during the Depression but we didn't know it."

Believe me Mama and I knew we were poor! Milk was five cents a quart and a quart lasted us a long time because Mama ate her oatmeal without milk so there would be more for me. We ate beans and potatoes. The beans were just plain beans with no meat to season them. Mama sometimes made little balls out of flour and water, kind of like dumplings, and then she boiled them in watered down canned milk. Canned milk never tasted like milk. The taste of canned milk has greatly improved since then. Mama never called this concoction she made soup. She called it graveyard stew. I guess I liked it because sometimes lately I've made some for myself but I couldn't get anyone else in my family to eat graveyard stew. Maybe I should have called it soup.

We had an enclosed back porch and when the milkman brought the milk, he sat our glass quart bottle on the outside windowsill along with our other perishables. It kept cold but didn't freeze because enough heat escaped from the window. I guess that is why our house was so hard to heat because so much heat escaped. The window made a good fridge though it looked funny with food sitting in the window. The milk bottle was bigger at the bottom and got smaller at the neck where thick yellow cream filled the whole top of the bottle. Mama nailed an orange crate across the window so she could open the window and reach the food. It was just like having a fridge.

There was a big spud field behind our house, full of nice big bakers. Mama went out one day to get a couple. The man who owned the field was one of the few wealthy men in town and he owned lots of property in Ashton and in Idaho Falls. When he saw Mama getting potatoes, he shot at her to scare her away. I thought that terrible man should have given her a sack of spuds. Mama would have given him spuds if he needed them. After that, we got them at night and got enough to last a while. Well, it was either that or do without.

Some of the neighbors were very kind to us and shared what they had. One even gave us an old radio when they got a new one. It was a long shaped box radio and a big horn speaker that sat on top of it. It squealed, squawked and whistled a lot but we could manage to hear Amos and Andy. Mama liked to listen to Amy McPherson, other preachers, and the hymns. She sang with them, "Onward Christian Soldiers" and "We Will Gather at the River." She had a very nice pleasant voice and I loved to hear her sing except for some of the high notes when I had to cover my ears. Mama sang a lot. I guess it helped her through the grief and sadness of her days.

Poor as we were I think the family across the street had even harder times than Mama and I did. There must have been five or six kids in that family and one little boy swallowed some lye that his mother used to make soap. Or, maybe she used it when she washed clothes. It seems to me they did put lye in the washing in those days but I can't understand why.

The boy was never able to swallow food after that so Dr. Spencer took him to the Spencer Hospital to live and he was there until he grew up. He had the run of the hospital and the best of care. Everyone felt so sorry for that family and helped them as much as they could. Seems to me people are not as interested in helping others now when they are having hard times as they used to be.

One day I saw the little girl playing with a stick of firewood. She had drawn a face on it and wrapped it in a cloth pretending it was a doll. I still had two or three of the dolls Santa had brought me over the years and I thought I was too big to play with dolls anyway.

"Mama, I want to give that little girl one of my dolls."

"That would be a very nice thing to do. Choose which one and I'll make some cute clothes and bonnets for her before you give her away."

I chose a doll that had a few cracks and wrinkles in her face due to the material used to make doll heads in those days, or maybe I got her too close to the stove. She was my favorite doll because of the flaws and I felt sorry for her having that imperfect face.

Mama went overboard with the new clothes and made the cutest things I had ever seen for a doll. When I put the lacey bonnet that Mama crocheted for her on her head and her pretty eyes peeked out from under it I felt like I couldn't give her up.

"She looks like she is going to cry Mama."

"Well you don't have to give her away if you don't want to."

I sure didn't want to but I did. The little girl was ecstatic and I felt wonderful.

After Roosevelt became president, there was more help for the desperately poor in the Depression years. God bless him. We were able to get what they called "relief" then. It is called welfare now. The food was called commodities and consisted of rancid butter, terrible tasting canned milk, old tasting salt pork. It wasn't really up to standard but I think it helped keep us from starving.

I've read that Mother Teresa said, "An easy way of life with no form of suffering has no depth."

Our way of life reached great depths during the next few years.

Chapter 25

During my early years when I lived in Ashton my favorite places to spend time were the library and the theater. The first movies I saw were silent and a lady sat in a pit at the floor of the movie screen and played a piano all through the show. At times the music would be soft and gentle and other times it was loud and fierce depending on the scenes being acted out on the screen. The expressions on the faces of the actors showed anger, love, fear or happiness. The motions of their hands and arms told the rest of the story, which was sometimes hilarious and sometimes sad. Mama read the captions on the screen to me before there were talkies.

I remember Charlie Chaplain with the baggy pants, the funny shoes, his round hat and the little black mustache but I remember the talking pictures much better because I was older then.

I especially liked the Tarzan movies. I thought life in the jungle with all the animals to be friends with would be a wonderful life. I guess Tarzan was my favorite but then again it may have been Rin Tin Tin. I really liked Jackie Cooper and his German Shepard dog.

I liked to see the news reels too because I learned about other places besides Idaho. I longed to go to those places and in my later life I got to fulfill some of those dreams.

I remember seeing two little princesses standing on a ship waving. They were about my age. One of them grew up to be the Queen of England and I always felt a fondness for her as I watched her grow up over the years because of seeing that news reel when she was a little girl princess.

In the lobby of the theater, there were big glamorous pictures in ornate frames of all the most popular stars. Theda Bari, Mae West, Wallace Berry, Janet Gaynor, Gloria Swanson, Lesley Howard. The women were so beautiful, and in the movies they lived in beautiful houses and wore lovely fur coats, long evening gowns and sparkling jewelry. The men were all so handsome and always dressed in their suits and ties except Wallace Berry. He was a comedian. The glamor was enough to make me know when I grew up I would go to Hollywood and be a movie star.

Sometimes after Papa had died, we didn't have a dime for the movie so I hung around the lobby after the others went in and the owner saw me giving him my most pitiful forlorn smile. I could tell he felt sorry for me.

"Why don't you go in and see the picture show and bring me a dime some other time?"

One day I made a special trip to give him the ten pennies I had saved up and he canceled the rest of my debt.

At the library, I could check out the "Little Big Books" and "Rebecca of Sunnybrook Farm" and of course again my favorite, the Tarzan books. I spent many hours there because the Librarian liked to discuss books with us and she told us stories. I still have my Ashton library card.

Mama put me in terrible long underwear and long stockings very early in the fall and those particular items of clothing really made me feel humble. I held the stockings up with a garter belt with straps over the shoulders to keep the belt from sliding down over my skinny hips. As soon as I got out of sight, I rolled the stockings down and the underwear up leaving the long garters to flop around under my dress. Mama was always afraid I would get cold but I would rather be cold than be so embarrassed with those long stockings when everyone else wore anklets.

I was one of those kids that had to wear black and white tennis shoes with white circles at the ankles. Recently, I've seen young people wearing the same type of tennis shoes because they wanted to. I wore them because they only cost about a dollar a pair. The first thing to go was always the laces and sometimes Mama sewed them back together but if there wasn't time she tied knots in them.

My feet sweat in those tennis shoes and one day the girl sitting in front of me turned around and pointed down at me feet.

"Your feet stink!"

When I told Mama, she scrubbed those stinky shoes up good. Maybe she put Lysol or something in the water anyway the soles started peeling away from the tops the next day at school and I came home flapping the soles as I walked. Mama went out to the shed. She got an old inner tube and then cut rubber bands out of them to put around the shoes to hold the soles on until she could get me another pair on payday.

I think Mama was old fashioned for the times. The clothes she wore were very plain but I think her clothes were more becoming than many of the funny styles we wear now. She had always worn clothes that covered women up pretty good and it was hard for her to adjust to the new fashions. In her pictures when she was young, she had very pretty clothes and hairstyles.

Women's clothes were going through the wonderful days of the flappers. Mabel wore short skirts with fringe and showed her knees off in silk stockings when she danced the Charleston. During my life I've seen many changes in fashion. I wrote this poem about all the changes I've lived through.

FASHION
I often have flashbacks to the styles of my past.
I remember all the fashions that never seemed to last.
I think about the latest styles that so often came and went.
It was hardly worth the money that we so freely spent.

Nothing lasts forever and we are lucky this is true.
I never did wear bustles like mother used to do.
I never wore high button shoes that you fastened with a hook.
They had thrown away the corsets for a new and modern look.

The roaring twenties brought about the fancy flapper girls.
They curled their hair with curling irons or cuter spit curls.

Short skirts, long beads and fringe were all the go.
And when they danced the Charleston a lot of leg would show.

We danced through the big band era in skirts they called swing.
There was music in our life and songs that we could sing.
We wore poodle skirts, bobby sox and saddle shoes.
We could jitterbug, waltz, or just listen to the blues.

Women started wearing pants and brought a brand new trend.
Like slacks, bell-bottoms and jeans you could hardly bend.
We wore pedal pushers, riding pants and pant suits with style.
Dresses almost disappeared from the fashion scene a while.

We've gone through mini-skirts, maxi-skirts and skirts in between.
Some new styles are pretty and some are most obscene.
The fashions lately are really bad and these are the facts.
I hate seeing armpits, belly buttons and especially buttcracks.

Chapter 26

I think I was around nine or ten when picture shows had become the joy of my life that Shirley Temple emerged as the most popular movie star in the world. What an adorable lovable child she was with her darling dimples her amazing talent and those bouncing ringlet curls.

Every little girl wanted Shirley Temple curls. Kids had been wearing their hair in straight cut off bangs or what they called a boyish bob or else we wore it in feathered style around our face.

I wanted a permanent wave like all the other kids so I could have Shirley Temple curls that would last. Mama had been wrapping my hair around rags to make the ringlets but they didn't last very long.

I imagine permanent waves cost around three or four dollars. I have no idea but Mama thought I should have a permanent wave too bless her heart. I hoped it didn't turn out in fuzzy curls like Mama's permanent wave did.

Mama led me to the Beauty Parlor and left me alone with the lady to get my permanent. The whole place smelled like my sister's baby's wet diapers. There was black hair mixed with other dirt swept into a pile near a big chair that leaned back and looked kind of like the chair at the barbershop. Over in the corner stood a spooky looking machine on a pole with a round top. There were clamps dangling on long electric wires from the top of the contraption. It had short legs that spread out at the bottom and there were little wheels at the ends of the legs. I began putting the whole picture together and that's when I first started getting scared. I realized that machine might have something to do with permanents. It looked dangerous. I wondered if the nearby door led out so I could escape from the room before the lady came back.

It was too late! The lady walked clomp clomp clomp over to me sitting in the big chair in front of a mirror and swung my chair around so I could see myself in the mirror and she could see me too.

"Hi Ruthie, I hear you want curly hair is that so?"

I don't know how she knew my name because I didn't know hers. She seemed so jolly but for some reason I didn't trust her.

"Yes, um maybe."

"Well let's see what we can do. She ran her fingers through my hair. Your hair is sure fine."

There were bottles, tubes, combs and brushes and hair rollers among the junk scattered on the table under the mirror. She pushed my head forward and washed it in a big wash pan then dried it with a bath towel very roughly until it was almost dry. She reached for a metal hair roller and a bottle from the table and spread the stuff from the bottle across the rod she had rolled a strand of my hair on. Right away I recognized it as the baby diaper smells in the room. I thought she would never stop jerking my head around and rolling my hair up. But, the worst was yet to come.

When she finally finished she walked over to the corner to a machine with dangling clamps hanging on electric wires. She held it by the pole and started rolling it toward me. She put a clamp on every one of the rods and I watched the whole procedure in the mirror. It took such a long time I worried I might wet my pants any minute.

Then she started the real torture in that old time beauty parlor torture chamber. She reached up above my head to a light fixture hanging from the ceiling. It had a dual plug with a light bulb in one side and she plugged the permanent wave machine in the other side.

"Now just sit there while the machine curls your hair. I'll be back in a few minutes to see if it's time to take the curling rods off."

Her shoes went clomp, clomp, clomp. I wondered, "How far away is she going anyway?"

I was alone with the monster of all monsters and tied down so couldn't get away. The diaper smell got stronger. The machine made a funny sound. It sounded like a sizzle. I wondered if it was smoking. How long is a few minutes? Maybe I should holler HELP!

Clomp, clomp, clomp, after an eternity she came clomping back into the room.

"Let's see if you're done yet."

She unrolled one curler a little way and decided it was time to remove all the clamps and rods so she reached up and unplugged the machine. As each curler came off cute little ringlets fell all over my head. But they were so little and looked nothing like I expected.

Just a couple of weeks before there had been a little girl in town that did an imitation of Shirley Temple. She had perfect curls and could sing and dance so you would hardly believe it wasn't the real Shirley Temple. That is exactly what I wanted to do.

"Shirley Temple has big bouncy ringlets. How come mine are so tiny?"

The lady laughed at my question and started brushing my ringlets. I walked out with fuzzy little curls just like Mama's.

I finally gave up permanents as old age crept nearer and I had started into my second childhood. After about ten years of beauty salons and forty years of using home permanents I went back to the bangs and boyish bob and feathered styles of my first childhood. I cut it myself so I don't ever have to go to the hair stylist's torture chamber again.

Chapter 27

I got my first job when I was about ten years old. The title of the job was picking up spuds. I worked after school and on Saturdays. Actually, it was pretty hard labor for a child and I'm not sure it paid for the shoes and socks and clothing I wore out working in those dirty hot fields. But still, it was fun and I look back with great pleasure to those lovely Indian summer days I spent in the spud fields around Ashton. I wouldn't trade them for any of the computer games I would be playing if I was a child growing up now in the computer age.

In fall after a frost killed the vines and they turned crisp and brown the spuds were dug with a spud digger. Nice big mostly perfect spuds lay on top of the ground drying off a few days until the pickers came to pick them. Big fields of spuds or onions make a very pretty picture in my mind. Especially since I know how much work goes into that picture.

We picked up spuds off the ground and put them in a heavy wire bushel basket with a handle on it. The grown-ups stooped down to pick up the spuds but kids usually sat on their backside and scooted along on the ground. It was a long time before the kids filled a basket. It got so heavy we could only drag it along and of course there were always those that had to start throwing clods or little spuds. That always caused some bawling and scolding and time out from work. Maybe we really played more than we worked.

When we finally filled the basket we drug it to where a grown-up emptied it into a gunny sack and a man loaded the full sack onto a truck. Most of the time they made us pick up a few more spuds to make a full basket before they would empty it.

I don't know why they were always called spuds in Idaho. There was a Spud Day celebration every year in Shelley, a town near Idaho Falls. Our school yearbook was called The Spud. I once had a job called cutting spuds where I sat at a table in a spud cellar and pulled a spud across an upright blade to cut spuds into planting sizes. There were jobs called sorting spuds and grading spuds. The farmers always had a spud cellar where they stored spuds to sort spuds or cut spuds and sometimes to hold spuds until they got a better price.

Spud cellars had a dank smell and most of the time there were a few rotten spuds around in the cellar some place. Funny how terrible they can smell.

The cellars were built by first digging out the cellar deep enough and wide enough to drive a loaded truck down the middle and pile spuds on both sides. Then the farmer went to the hills and cut poles to make a few feet tall rounded top over the cellar and piled straw on top of the poles. He piled the dirt he had dug out for the cellar over the straw. The temperature inside kept about the same all the time and was perfect for keeping spuds. Lately I feel like they are kept for a very long time. Too long I think. Sometimes I can smell that dank cellar smell on them.

Kids liked to get on top of spud cellars. One time my sister's little boy was playing there when an airplane came swooping down close to the spud cellar right toward him. He was afraid the airplane would hit him and it looked big. He screamed so loud they almost thought the plane had hit him and everyone came running.

He explained, "I was so scared I decided to run but I didn't know which way to run so I ran both ways and fell down."

People all over the world know that Idaho is famous for potatoes or spuds as we called them. The volcanic ash in the soil around the Snake River is perfect for growing potatoes. The farms with irrigation raised the best spuds in the world. The spuds I buy at the grocery store now are not even close in quality to the ones that came from Idaho in those days where number one really meant number one. Spuds that were graded number one had to be a certain uniform size with no imperfections like knobs, bruises, dark spots, blemishes, or gouged places caused by the way they are harvested now.

The farmer was docked for the whole sack if culls hadn't been sorted out before they were bagged. Now I've been told the stores are allowed a few culls in a bag of number ones.

Growing spuds was quite a demanding and time consuming occupation for the farmer and his family. The ground was worked and then spuds were planted by a potato planting machine behind a tractor in raised rows building a trench for the water to run between the rows. This method of watering kept the water off the vines and in the ground.

The water was brought from the river to the farmer by digging a canal and then each farmer was allotted a certain amount of water. He often had to get up in the middle of the night and go close or open a head gate when his time for using the water was up. He wore high irrigation boots and carried a shovel to repair leaks or change direction of the flow.

The farmers in the valley along the Snake River pumped water from the river into the canals and then they pumped the water from the canals into the irrigation ditches on their farms.

Having enough water at the right time was a very important part of growing their crops. I don't know if anyone ever got killed over water rights but I heard there were threats by gun toting farmers.

Some farmers used more than their share of allotted water and this caused bitter disputes and hard feelings among all the farmers. They formed an organization for controlling the water and hired a man to oversee and regulate the water rights of each of the farmers. They furnished a place for him to live nearby and he made regular rounds overseeing his territory. This was very effective in protecting the use of the water but I wonder if some years he made more money than the farmers made.

Talk to any old time spud farmer and he will tell you due to modern technology, insecticides and fertilizer the good russet spuds I picked on my first job are not the same as the tasteless spuds we are buying to eat now. The russet potatoes that Idaho is famous for were one of Luther Burbank's experiments in developing better plants.

Mama, my niece Dollie Jo and me, behind our house in Ashton.

Playing in the snow in Ashton.

People from all over the world came to the Ashton Dog Derby.

Local woman racing the in the dog derby.

Chapter 28

One summer when I was around eleven years old Mama got a job cooking for the men who were cutting lodge poles to build a recreation pavilion in Idaho Falls. This was a W.P.A. project which was sponsored by the government during the depression years to give unemployed men jobs during those hard times.

Mama's job took us to a place a few miles from Ashton which was called Big Falls in those days but later the name was changed to Mesa Falls. Another waterfall a short distance away was called Little Falls but now it is Lower Mesa Falls. These two beautiful falls are located on the North Fork of the Snake River.

During the summer she worked there we lived in a large inn called Big Falls Inn which was originally built by Mesa Power Company. It was intended as an office building for the power company but was later made into an inn. As I remember, there were five bedrooms upstairs. It had a huge main room downstairs with fireplaces at each end of the room. The fireplaces were built with large smooth round stones. I guess the main room was intended as a lounge and a place to dance. It had a lovely hardwood floor.

The rest of the downstairs' rooms consisted of a large dining room with a long table and a fully equipped restaurant style kitchen with big pots and pans hanging over the worktable. The huge wood burning stove occupied one whole wall. The dishes were thick heavy white platters and thick white mugs like were often found in restaurants. I helped Mama do the dishes so I remember how many there were and how heavy.

This was truly a great place to spend the summer if it hadn't been for the dishwashing routine once a day. Thank goodness the men ate breakfast and supper at home.

I felt as though I was in the movies living is such a palatial palace.

It wasn't hard to make believe I lived in a castle with the two other princesses that I had seen on the news reel at the picture show in Ashton.

Mama and I had the whole place to ourselves except for the foreman of the WPA project. Mr. Causey had been the long time caretaker of the inn and was famous for his hospitality especially his cooking, gambling and homemade spirits.

Mama, who was afraid of gypsies and lightning, was also afraid of everything and everybody, including Mr. Causey. Every night when we went to bed she stuck a big butcher knife in the frame of the door and across the door as a lock to keep everything and everybody out. Then she leaned a high back chair under the doorknob so the door couldn't be pushed open just in case the knife didn't hold. I was glad I had such a careful Mama to take care of me. I always felt safe in the little room we shared with the butcher knife in the door.

There was no electricity at the inn because at that time it was a remote area. We used kerosene lamps just like the ones we had on the dry farm when we lived there.

Mr. Causey had to carry water uphill from the river for use in the house and for the men to wash up with at the washstand outside the kitchen door. He used a heavy wooden yoke across his shoulders with a bucket hanging on each side. He was a big sturdy man but I'm sure after that summer he really had big muscles. Of course, we had to be very conservative with water but it took a lot cooking for that many men and washing the dishes.

Mama and I took our clothes down by the river and washed them on the rocks. We felt like pioneers but I remember it as a lot of fun there beside a shallow place making a sudsy wash basin in the cold water and dipping our clothes up and down. The sound the water made as it cascaded down 114 feet from the top of the waterfall blended with bluebird songs.

We spread our clothes on nearby bushes to dry in the sun and sat there on rocks hidden in the tall grass enjoying the moments of a wonderful summer day. As we relaxed in that picturesque setting and I glanced across the river I could see the swinging bridge that Mama wouldn't let me cross over to the other side on.

"No, don't ever get on that swinging thing! It looks like it's about to come loose and go plunging over the falls."

Right then and there I plotted to go on the bridge some time when she wasn't around. Mama always kept a pretty close eye on me and she would suddenly pop up at unexpected moments to see what I was doing especially if there were strangers around. I did get about half way across the bridge one day and it started swinging so I turned around and by the time I made it back to safety it was jumping so much I could hardly keep my footing. Mama was right.

There was a windup victrola in the big recreation room and lots of old scratchy records. They were songs I had never heard before but I soon learned them. I spent much of my time playing the victrola and singing old-fashioned songs. Much to my disappointment that wonderful machine broke after a few weeks. But, I still have those songs to sing and I still pull them out of the recesses of that time of my life and sing them. Much as I want to I can't carry a tune and my son and granddaughter always start moaning when I want to sing one of those old songs to them.

That summer I had my mind set on a pair of riding pants and boots. I had seen someone in the movies I think it was Greta Garbo or Katharine Hepburn riding a horse all decked out in those pants that flared out at the hips and tapered down to a snug fit at the legs where they met the boots. In my dream I visualized those boots all shiny and brown and the tan pants set off with a white turtle-neck sweater.

Every time Mr. Causey went to town for supplies he asked me what I would like for him to bring home to me. I always said riding pants and boots and he always laughed but never brought them. Usually he brought a bag of candy. One time on his return from town he brought me a sweet little pink organdy ruffled dress with little flowers embroidered on it. It looked suitable for a four year old in my mind. I never wore it as I felt too grown up for such a baby's dress. When he asked me why I never wore it I said I was saving it for special. I was a tomboy and not the frilly dress type at all. Riding pants and boots were more my style.

Big Falls was such a beautiful area and of course it drew tourists from all over the United States. At least the ones brave enough to venture down the steep rough road that led to it. Once they started down there was no place to turn around and they always complained to

Mama about the road.   Usually the tourists were on their way to
Yellowstone Park and saw Big Falls on the map not realizing how hard
it was to get down to the falls on that road.

Sparkling water and the rainbows in the mist over the falls were a
sight to behold as they danced in the sunlight and they were well worth
the difficulty of the journey.

One day a car with a license plate from Rhode Island drew the
attention of one of the natives of Idaho that lived around there.

"Rody Is Land, hum, Rody Is Land, where is that?"

Everyone laughed but I'm sure the tourists thought we were a
bunch of hillbillies living back in that remote area.

One time a drunk guy made it down the hill okay but went
staggering close to the cliff and fell from the top of the falls almost all
the way to the bottom where he landed on a big rock.   It was very
difficult and dangerous for the people who volunteered to climb down
there and bring him up.   When they carried him out he was wearing a
big silly grin and not in the least bit hurt.   Mr. Causey saw how worried
I was.

"Don't worry Ruthie, he was too drunk to feel anything."

The horses the men used to get the lodge poles out of the woods
were left in the barn over the weekend.   The men commuted each day
from Idaho Falls in a big truck but had the weekends off.

One weekend I thought what fun it would be to ride one of the
horses down to Little Falls and over the scenic trails around there.
There were four nice old gentle plugs so I chose one of the smaller
horses and spent a very happy Sunday afternoon riding bareback over
the trails.   I can't remember if I had gotten Mama's approval or not but
probably not.   When I put away the horse I neglected to shut and lock
the barn door securely.   All four horses got out that night and
wandered several miles down the hills towards town.   The men spent
most of the next day trying to find all the horses and bring them back.
I can't remember if there was a scolding but I really felt terrible about
the trouble I caused.

A big black bearskin hung on the side of the garage.   It was such
an ugly thing hanging there and though I often glanced at it I avoided
going near it.   It seemed so undignified for a bear.   The live ones I had
seen always carried their heads high and proud.

Then one day, when I was throwing out the dishwater, I threw my ring away in the water and while I was looking for it I got close to the bear hide. I saw it was absolutely crawling with bedbugs. Bedbugs were common household pests in those days. Lots of homes were infested with them but people never let anyone know they had them because it was considered to be so disgraceful and definitely a sign of uncleanliness.

Bedbugs sometimes lived in the pine trees. They got on the birds and the birds would nest in the attics of houses. The bugs spread through the house making it their permanent living quarters and using humans for their source of nourishment.

Mama fought them with everything she had. Finally, they were more or less eliminated when DDT came into use which I guess turned out to be much more harmful to us than the bugs. We just had to tolerate a lot of pesky things in those days before DDT. Anyway, Mama thought that weeds and bugs were put here to keep us humble.

Mama devised a plan when she planted a garden. She put four seeds in each hill. One seed for the neighbors, one for us, one to rot and one for the bugs and it all seemed to work out fine with that plan.

Chapter 29

I've been back to Big Falls several times. The last time I was there I couldn't find my name where I wrote it on the front porch on one of the logs more than eighty years ago. The tree where Papa carved his name when we used to go there camping and fishing had been cut down but it had stood there announcing his presence in that location for a good share of my life.

One of the times I was there the lodge had been converted into a Boy Scouts Camp. It was such a perfect place for scouts. I could imagine them exploring all the places I explored and hiking all the trails I had hiked. Each time I returned that big house had shrunk to a much smaller size than I remembered and each time it had deteriorated.

Mesa Falls is one of nature's masterpieces and I am glad that it has never been exploited as a multi-use recreation area. The electric company from the east that built the lodge eventually intended it to be a rental property. The rich and powerful owners of the company often flew from back east to use it as a vacation spot. I heard some of the parties in those days during the twenties were pretty wild. They intended to harness the falls for electric power but the plan never materialized. This is one of the stories I've heard but the property has changed hands so many times over the years who knows which stories are the true ones.

I don't know why all the many plans fell through so now Mesa Falls is the only falls in Idaho that hasn't been harnessed for an electric power plant.

I believe the story that the Hendricks family originally homesteaded 160 acres in the Mesa Falls area in 1901 is true. They paid $1.25 an acre and built a cabin 200 feet from the falls. Clara Hendricks thought it was a dangerous place for their four children and couldn't wait to move away.

One of my visits to my castle by the falls turned out to be one of the saddest memories I carried with me for several years. First, I was shocked by the neglected grounds and over-grown mess as we drew close to the lodge. Next, I saw the bearskin was hanging in shreds on rotting logs of the garage. The lodge had practically fallen down and it was too dangerous to explore inside. The hardwood floors were gone. They had fallen to the ground below. There were bats and rats and skunks. It smelled of skunks. The skunks had taken up residence in my castle in those spacious rooms where I spent that lovely summer when I was eleven years old. The sad scene filled my heart with sorrow.

But, this story has a happy ending in many ways. About twenty years later I returned once again to that magic place. The first thing I noticed was how the road had been changed. It took a more gradual way down and there were no ruts and rocks and bumps. The barn and garage and pitiful bearskin were gone entirely and a rather large parking lot took their place. There right before my eyes appeared my castle the same as it looked when I lived in it. In this era it probably wouldn't look like much to most people compared to the fancy lodges now surrounding that area but it is one of my most important memories.

I can no longer hike the trails or walk to see the falls but I have a scooter that takes me most places I want to go. They have built ramps, great boardwalks and viewing platforms at Mesa Falls and the rainbows still dance in the mist.

I couldn't keep from telling the group of people admiring the falls that I used to live in the lodge. It seemed like it still belonged to me just as it did so many years before and I was proud of it and wanted everyone to know.

We discovered the area now belonged to the Targhee US Forest Service and the lodge is on the Registry of Historic Places. I'm so happy that the people caring for my castle love it as much as I did.

We entered the lodge by the back door where the kitchen used to be. I looked for the big cook stove where Mama cooked those wonderful meals for the WPA workers. I could hear them complimenting her and see Mama and me working together at the big sink washing dishes or hanging big kettles to dry.

Everything was gone from the kitchen. The stove no longer took up half the space and big kettles weren't hung over the workbench. In their places were tables with displays of furs and skulls and bones from animals that lived in that part of the country. Cougars, coyotes, bears, weasels and others were there to view and learn about.

The dining room was a hallway and office space which led to the great room where I used to play the victrola in the big empty dance hall. Nice seating arrangements were in front of both fireplaces. The ranger sat at a desk in the middle of the room.

I let her know I used to live there and she became very excited. She asked me questions and wanted know if I had any pictures of that time. She asked me if I remembered Charlie Causey and lots of questions about him and about the history of the area. I didn't remember most of the things she wanted to know. She had worked on the renovation and did research for ten years and she told me lots of things I didn't know.

One question has kept me puzzled ever since then.

"Was there just a dirt floor in the kitchen when you lived here?"

I can't remember for sure but it seems way back in my mind there is a memory of a dirt floor. That doesn't seem like something anyone would forget. So, I don't know if she planted that memory with suggestion or if there really was a dirt floor. My wonderful memory has failed to convince me one way or the other.

My castle, Big Falls Inn

Chapter 30

That summer when Mama cooked for the men who were getting the lodge poles for the pavilion in Idaho Falls my life changed completely. This was the second big change in my eleven years. The first change was after Papa's death when we had suffered such grief, sorrow and poverty.

One day in late summer a very distinguished looking man with gorgeous silver-streaked hair, a kind, happy face and a slight limp came to the lodge.

"Hi! I'd like to order lunch. Just some bacon and eggs would be fine. I see you aren't ready for lunch yet. You probably don't get many people in here. That road down is a real problem. Why don't they fix it? Someone told me about the falls so I came down to see them."

Mama laughed, "Well no, I'm not ready for lunch because this isn't a restaurant. I cook for some men that are getting logs out but they have the weekends off so they aren't here today. I was about to make some sandwiches for my daughter and me. I can make one for you too and we can share our lunch with you."

I think Mama took a shine to that man right away. I know I did and now that I think about it I think he probably came to see the pretty widow woman he heard about and not the falls.

Mama's sandwiches turned out to be quite a spread and I know she hadn't planned that kind of lunch for just the two of us. She sliced off thick slices of roast beef and made hot beef sandwiches on her own baked bread. She warmed up some mashed potatoes and covered everything in rich brown gravy. The apple cobbler drowning in thick whipped cream couldn't keep from winning any man's heart.

The type of work Bill had done during his life took him many exciting places and he had lots of interesting tales to tell. He had previously worked drilling for oil in the oil fields of Texas. That was how he had gotten his limp because he was blown several feet in the air when an oil well exploded. He let me feel the pebbles that were still in his knee. It was a strange sensation because I could feel the pebbles roll when I touched them. It made me shudder to think there were rocks in his legs. It felt a lot worse than my knee replacement feels when I rub it.

He changed jobs after the accident in the oil fields and now he was employed by the Bureau of Reclamation as a diamond driller. He explained that on his job as a diamond driller he used a big pressure drill to remove cores of rock from deep in the earth to determine if the rock formation and the surrounding ground would be suitable for building a dam. It is very important to locate dams where the rock is stable and will hold the great pressure created by the back-up of water.

The drill is fitted with black diamonds. Diamonds are so hard they will cut through the hardest rock thus his title of diamond driller.

Bill was working nearby on a dam site on the Teton River. His job was almost finished in this location and his superior, a geologist, had determined this was not a suitable site to build a dam. This later proved to be an accurate assessment and though it was definitely recommended not to build a dam in that location some years later the government put a dam there anyway. The earth-filled dam hadn't completed finished filling when it broke and flooded many square miles all the way to Rexburg several miles away. It destroyed homes and property in the path of the rushing water. I wasn't living in Idaho at the time so I don't remember if lives were lost but it seems there would have been. The floodwaters came through the Teton River that flowed behind our dry farm where we lived on Hog Hollow Rd. many years before.

Mama and I listened all afternoon to Bill's interesting life stories and Mama told him her life stories, mostly about Oregon. Mama said, "Oh my goodness look at the time. Well, I might as well fix something for you to eat before you go."

Bill responded with a twinkle in his eye and I could see he was delighted she asked him to stay longer.

"Alright but please don't go to any trouble cooking. Just what you happen to have is fine."

Mama wasn't going to pass up this chance to show off her culinary skills again so we had to wait a long time for her to prepare dinner. I think she believed that old saying that the way to a man's heart is through his stomach.

Bill and I talked while Mama put together her culinary skills. It was during this time I started wishing he would be my new Dad.

Bill returned again the next weekend and enjoyed another meal with us. A short time later we had another visit from him and after several of these visits he suggested we spend our life with him. This proposal made me very happy. I had already began to think of him as our knight in shining armor who had come riding up in a white car to our castle to rescue us from the unknown future we had ahead. I thought Bill was a wonderful man and I loved him already. I was sure he would make Mama's life easier and happier. Besides, I saw my dream of riding pants and boots with the white turtleneck sweater coming true. I could see he had money and riding around Island Park, Henry's Fork, and Pond's Lodge in his big luxury car was truly a joyful experience for me.

Mama recently had a letter that our house in Ashton was going to be sold for the back taxes she owed. I guess the taxes were two or three hundred dollars. She had already lost the farm after Papa's death. She wouldn't have a place to live before long. No one could ever take Papa's place in her heart but I guess maybe she thought Bill was a nice man and a way out of the uncertainty of her future.

Mama packed everything she could in her big old dome top trunk. These were keepsakes from her whole life. They included the pictures I have now, some of them over a hundred years old, also the lovely brown swatch of her hair she had cut during the twenties when women first bobbed their hair. There was her marriage license, her diploma, our report cards that she was so proud of, other important papers and the few clothes we had. My sister Mabel took some of her other things including the nice mahogany piano and other furniture salvaged from better times.

I went shopping for my riding pants and boots and we were on our way to sunny California to Bill's next dam drilling project.

Mama told her friends goodbye and laughing she said, "Send me a box of snowballs sometime. I'm going to California where the sun shines and it's warm all the time and I'm afraid I'll miss the snow."

Chapter 31

Much to our surprise Truckee, California had as much or more snow than we left behind in Idaho. Can you imagine my disappointment? I expected to see orange trees with oranges on them even in the winter and bowers of flowers that bloom in the sun and a sun kissed miss like in the song "California Here I Come" which we sang all the way to California. My riding pants and boots seemed a little out of place in my snowy new home.

That wasn't the only disappointment that we had. Bill couldn't work in all that snow and after a few months he had to sell the beautiful white car that he came riding up in to rescue Mama and me from a fate worse than death. My new friends had decided we were very rich when they saw that car but my esteem went down several notches when the car went. Bill had to go to work on the WPA. My brother decided to come and live with us. He couldn't find a job either. Bill now had three extra mouths to feed. Bill was such a good man.

Mama wasn't much better off than she had been in Idaho. We did have a very nice upstairs apartment and the man that worked with Bill had the downstairs apartment. His wife was pregnant and he had two other children around my age so it was even more difficult for their family. Jane and Warren, Les' children, became my very good friends as we traveled from one job to another over the next few years. It was almost like having another brother and sister.

The snow finally melted enough so everyone could go back to work. Life was great. We got another car. Not as nice as the big white car, but it took us sightseeing every weekend.

Truckee looked like a very old town but it had burned down several times and the new buildings were built to look like old ones. The railroad had a roundhouse where the trains came in to add on another engine to help pull the train over the Donner Pass in the Sierra

Mountains. Out of town a ways was a tunnel made with boards to keep the snow from drifting over the tracks. I think it is still there.

I grew to love my new home and it didn't take long for me to settle into a whole new lifestyle. I liked my new school so much I could hardly wait to go to school each morning. The kids were so friendly I felt accepted right from the first.

There were two boys that liked me. One day Ernest gave me a note.

"Which one do you like best, me or Jack?

Next time I saw him I pointed my finger at him. "You."

He was my first boyfriend.

Our house sat on a curve on Main St. so we had a good view of downtown. Mama could watch Ernest and me when he came to walk with me to the movies. She watched again when we walked home. She never knew he sat with his arm around me in the movie house.

Ernest was very good looking and the most popular boy in our school. He wore nice wool shirts and the thing I remember most about him was that he smelled like ivory soap. I guess he washed his wool shirts in ivory soap. But he was fickle, and after a few months he dumped me for another new girl in school. Years later I learned Ernest lost a leg in World War II.

The schoolhouse was condemned that year because it was so old. We moved into the ski pavilion on the hill across the Truckee River. What a great place to go to school every day. We wore a ski suit over our clothes so we could ski after school. We wore our ski boots all day. Our ski suits didn't look anything like the ones now. They were wool and had elastic around the bottom of the puffy legs to keep the snow out. They had a matching ski jacket.

There was a tall ski jump built out of lumber beside the pavilion where competitions were often held. People came from everywhere to watch and to compete.

I never got up enough courage to climb up there so high and ski down the jump-off but lots of kids did.

On Saturdays we often tied our sleds on the back of a passing car and it pulled us up to Donner Lake where we skated. I know the way it is now with all the traffic that it's hard to believe. But at that time there were only a few cars and not many summer homes, just a few, mostly belonging to movie stars. We often saw someone we recognized from the movies when they visited Truckee and Lake Tahoe and Donner Lake.

Once the group of girls I hung out with heard Mae West was staying at the hotel downtown so we hurried down there after school. We peeked in the big hotel window and then the front door and there she sat in the lobby just as gorgeous as she looked on the movie screen. She was holding a cigarette in a long black cigarette holder. The smoke circled above her platinum blonde hair. Her lips were painted bright red and her eyes were heavy with black mascara. She saw us and when she smiled at us her cheeks turned to dimples. She motioned for us to come in. We just stood there in a huddle and giggled. She walked over to the door but we ran and I don't know why.

I remember a funny incident that happened when Bill's co-worker Les and his family and our family went to Donner Lake to fish through a hole in the ice. At least I thought it was funny even if I was the only one that laughed.

We built a huge bonfire on the lakeshore to roast weenies and make coffee and hot chocolate. We were all closely gathered around the fire trying to cook our own food and enjoying our moments of togetherness when suddenly tragedy struck.

Lester's wife had a red fox fur that she was very proud of and wore around her neck every place she went. It was a gift from her husband and she loved showing it off.

I didn't like it because it looked so real. It still had all its body parts like the head with the beady eyes and its dangling legs. The mouth had a clamp that she clamped one leg in to fasten the poor animal around her neck.

She swung around to put out the blaze on her marshmallow and caught the fox's bushy tail on fire from a sudden leaping flame in the bonfire.

Everyone started yelling, "You're on fire." Like she didn't already know it.

She ran in circles swatting at the fox's tail until Les caught her and jerked the firey fox from around her neck and doused it in the hole in the ice where we had been fishing. She stood there dangling the wet singed fox in her hand her face wet with tears and it was a pitiful sight to see. She started crying. "Oh God, my beautiful fox look at it. All the fur is singed off his tail. I wonder if I can get a new tail put on."

I don't know why I thought it was funny. I started laughing uncontrollably. Mama shushed me and took me to the car to explain how rude I had been to laugh. My laughter was contagious though and she started laughing uncontrollably too, until tears rolled down her face.

Chapter 32

It is hard to say which was more fun in Truckee, winters or summers. Both seasons had so many things to offer to children who like to be outdoors.

I learned to swim in the Truckee River. I'm not sure Mama knew how treacherous that river was or she wouldn't have let me near it I'm sure. It had deep holes with whirlpools and strong currents that swirled and rushed over big rocks.

There was one perfect swimming hole. Nearby was an old sawmill sawdust pile that had been smoldering for years but you couldn't tell it was still hot from the ground on top. I ran right in to it and burned my legs. They were not really bad burns so Mama never found out about it. I made sure she didn't see some of the blisters. Someone told me to put butter on them so I did. I don't think it helped.

During the summer months, the kids I ran around with spent the whole day roaming the hills around Truckee or else we were down by the Truckee River. We liked to snoop around the backyards of the houses on the river. We especially teased the peacocks that lived in one backyard. They spread their beautiful tail feathers and strutted around in circles for us. We all had vases full of peacock plumes in our homes.

My best friend Clair and I often visited an old German man who lived down by the river. He was a friend of her family who I think was German too. He fixed us German sausage and sauerkraut on black bread, which I had never seen before. There were always cheeses of all kinds and one of them was limburger cheese, which was one of my favorites, except it smelled like stinky feet. It is hard to find limburger cheese now and I think a lot of people haven't even heard of it. He gave us a half glass of dark ale to wash it down with but I didn't like it so I only took a sip and poured it down the sink when he went out of the room. I don't know why I didn't want him to know I didn't like it but I knew Mama would have a fit if she ever found out he gave us ale. I think that was why I didn't like it.

I don't remember his name but we always called him The Jeweler because he owned a jewelry store. He gave Clair and me each a gold chain with a little gold ball on it and I treasured that gift for many years as a keepsake of that nice old man.

Some years ago when TV had delightful shows to watch I used to watch Bonanza faithfully. It was filmed around the area where I had played when I was eleven and twelve and I often recognized my playgrounds in the some of the scenes that were filmed there.

There were wonderful big boulders in the surrounding hills to explore and meadows where violets grew. The ponderosa pine towered everywhere and by Donner Lake there were still the tall stumps where the Donner Party spent that horrible winter. Some of the boulders showed black smoke stains where the Donner Party built fires close against them to reflect the heat. The stumps have been placed inside a building now to preserve them.

The railroad tracks were by the river and hobos had camps there. These men were from other states and rode in the boxcars on freight trains to California. They were decent family men who had left their families to try to find work during the depression. They never caused any trouble and I guess children were safe around them because they sure didn't bother us any. They used to talk to us and tell us about their kids who were our age and how much they missed them. The big kettle of stew sitting on the bonfire smelled wonderful. They had gathered food by bumming it from people and shared it with each other. Seems to me people were more willing to help each other in those hard times.

Maybe I'm wrong but it seems to me people nowdays don't have much compassion for others and think they should pull themselves up by their bootstraps which is pretty hard to do if you don't have any boots.

The hobos used to come to our house asking for work like chopping wood or washing windows for food. Mama always gave them something until someone told her they marked the houses that always gave them food even if they didn't have any work. If she didn't have any work for them she didn't give any food after that. She figured the woman that told her that and other houses around should help too and the men could go there once in a while. Which they did.

I will call my friends my group instead of my gang because a gang now has somewhat different meaning than it did during that time in my life. I guess there were gangs in big cities but in the small towns I grew up our gangs were more like Our Gang in the movies. We were just fun little gangs of kids like Alfalfa and Spanky.

We were given a lot of freedom, and spent our days with no adult supervision. It seems to me by example, and by being taught, children may have had better values and morals and more self-discipline in those days, and we held onto these beliefs through our lives. The things we did might not have been too safe but we learned what not to do.

Kids were taught to show more respect for other people especially elders, teachers and policemen and though there were those who broke laws and had low morals and never practiced self-discipline it seems as though now there is an epidemic of unacceptable behavior by adults and children right here in the best country on earth. This land is our land and we want it back where it's safe for children to play all day wherever they are and go to school in a safe place.

Chapter 33

Bill loved to take us places and show us new things and we got to go to Sacramento several times and explore the sights. It was the biggest city I ever remember being in and every time we went we ate abalone either in a restaurant or in a tourist cabin we rented. Bill loved to cook them himself and bought them in the shell. They became my idea of the most supreme food in the world and now most people don't even know what they are. Abalone are a delightful shellfish like clams and oysters only bigger and better. The inside of the shell has beautiful colors and is often made into jewelry, usually necklaces or pins.

Tourist cabins were nothing like the motels we stay in now. They were individual cabins usually with two rooms and a bath. Old fashioned kitchens with stoves to cook on and lumpy cots and beds to sleep in. It was fun but more work than eating in a nearby café like we do now.

Reno was about thirty miles from Truckee along a road that wound its way beside the Truckee River. The first time I saw the super highway there now full of fast traffic I almost wept. Gone is the lovely drive and you can't take your eyes off the road long enough to enjoy the scenery. I pulled over in a wayside to let cars by my motor home and couldn't get back on the road for all the speeding traffic.

When we lived in Truckee we went to Reno every Saturday to shop and to sightsee. I loved the big chunks of milk chocolate sold in the bulk which I liked to eat with a banana in one hand and the chunk of chocolate in the other hand on the way home. That weekly habit was my downfall and I became a chocoholic and still suffer from that addiction to this very day.

We ate in a different ethnic restaurant every week and I learned to like foods from other countries almost as much as the moose meat and trout in Idaho. Mama on the other hand didn't care for some of the strange tasting food I especially enjoyed. In the Greek restaurant our waiter seemed very friendly and eager to please. He stopped beside our table.

"May I get you anything? How was your dinner? Was everything alright?"

"No it wasn't! This has to be the worst meal I ever ate in my life."

"I'm sorry. What was wrong with it?"

Mama started naming off a long list of disparaging comments about the food and in very descriptive terms.

I slunk down in my seat trying to hide I was so embarrassed. I couldn't believe it was my gentle Mama. It didn't seem like the same person that kept telling me over and over never to be impolite to people. We left and I don't know if we had to pay for her meal or not. I doubt it.

The sign across the middle of town is the only thing that remains the same in Reno. I think it is a wonderful sign. It says everything I want to say about Reno, "The Biggest Little City in the World."

Truckee is surrounded by the most beautiful scenery in the whole state of California. The Sierra Mountains are gorgeous both summer and winter. Lovely wildflowers bloom in the summer and snow sports bloom in winter bringing people from all over to enjoy the ski slopes and ice skating on Donner Lake or Lake Tahoe. Nearby Squaw Valley has been host to the Winter Olympics.

The snow comes down in big fluttering flakes and piles snow several feet high overnight. The next day the sun shines with such brilliance the glistening snow almost blinds you. It is truly a winter wonderland. I don't remember that we ever had blustering blizzards there like we had in Idaho. There seemed to be such a gentle peacefulness that hovered over Truckee in winter.

The dam site for Boca Dam where Bill was working was one of those pretty, peaceful places and in the summer Mama and I often went to work with him and spent the day there. We had picnic lunches, roamed around the area and waded in the little brook that flowed nearby. The water only came up to a little above our knees and the water was so clear you could see to the bottom. There were little fish swimming around our legs. Those little buggers must have thought Mama's varicose veins were worms and they started nibbling at them.

We watched Bill and Les drilling and bringing up cores from deep down in the bedrock. The cores were about a foot or so long and fascinating. They contained samples of different colored layers from past eras in time. The cores were given to the site geologist Mr. Gosset to study and these cores determined if this was a suitable site for a dam.

The diamond drill was powered by water being pumped from the stream. It came back out of the hole they were drilling in a hose with a terrific force. One day Mr. Gosset's daughter who was visiting from Nevada picked up the hose and was shooting it around knocking down bushes and digging up rocks and dirt with the powerful force of the water. I guess it was an accident but she hit me full blast right in my stomach with that stream of water. It knocked me down. I had on a swimming suit and it felt like it stripped the skin off the bare parts of my body. It was very painful but wasn't as bad as I thought when it first hit me so I got up.

"For crying out loud what are you trying to do kill me? Here give me that hose and let's see how you like it."

She apologized and then I apologized for getting mad. We hugged. After all, we were best friends.

There was only one thing I really wanted that I didn't already have. Well, maybe two things. I so wanted a bicycle to ride around to all the nice places there were to go and I wanted a dog. I had always had dogs. They were constant companions that I could tell my troubles to when I felt sad or lonely. They always loved me even when I didn't deserve it.

Mama explained why I shouldn't have either a dog or a bike.

"We can't acquire a lot of things because we will be moving to different places. We can't have a lot of stuff to move. How would we take a bike? Bill expects to be finished working here soon and we will be renting every place we go so we probably can't have a dog. It's hard to find a place where they allow dogs especially where we have to have a furnished place. Some landlords don't even want kids."

Well I thought that was the end of that but about a week or so later a little fluffy white half-grown puppy came and settled in on our back porch. To my surprise first thing Mama said was, "Poor little guy. Looks like he is hungry. I'll fix him some of that stew we had left over."

After he gobbled down the stew he showed her how cute he could be. He wiggled and twisted and wagged his tail like he was performing for Mama's eyes alone and she fell for it. I could tell.

It was time for me to put on my cute act too and maybe she would say, "Let's keep him."

"Isn't he the cutest little dog you ever saw? He is so cuddly and soft. He sure loves you Mama. Look how his eyes are always on you. He wants you to pet him. See how he follows everywhere you go. Can we keep him? He would be company for you when I'm at school. He is so little he wouldn't be hard to take along when we moved."

Mama reached down and actually picked him up and I had never seen her ever touch one of the dogs when we lived on the farm.

"There there little fella. You're going to be alright. He probably belongs to somebody. We will keep him until his owner shows up."

There was something extra special about that puppy. He seemed like one of the fluffy snowflakes that had come down from heaven just for me. "I'm going to call him Snowflake, Mama. He is as white as the snow and so fluffy."

In the days that followed the little dog and I bonded. I knew I could never give him up. He turned out to be such a good little pal and playmate. He twisted and wiggled every day when I came home from school he was so happy to see me, and so eager to play.

Mama thought dogs should always sleep in their own beds and his bed was in the basement. He didn't like it down there all alone and whined a little but he got used to it before long. It was cozy there by the furnace and he had a place to go to the bathroom and didn't have to go out in the snow. He was so smart and house trained he went and sat by the basement door when he wanted to go to the basement.

I worried for about a month about the owners showing up and then I decided he was mine for keeps it had been such a long time. Surely if he had a home the people would have come for him by now. Bill had posted a sign on the bulletin board in the Post Office in the lost and found section.

Snowflake and I were out on the front porch the day the owners came driving by. A woman dressed in a spiffy fur coat jumped out of the passenger side and called, "Here Tiny! Here Tiny! Come here,

Tiny baby."

My first thought was what a dumb name she's calling my dog. Then I realized what was going on so I grabbed Snowflake. That woman ran right up on the porch and took him from me and ran back to the car and that was the end. I never saw my dog again.

Chapter 34

I can only remember one kid in Truckee that had a bicycle. It seems strange that there weren't more because bicycles had been around for a long time and I know I sure wanted one. Why didn't other kids want one too?

That one bike belonged to a friend of mine so I kept after him to let me ride it. He was very reluctant but I was bigger than he was so I finally talked him into letting me ride it one day.

Now, I had never been on a bike before in my life and I thought you just got on it and rode. All you had to do was pedal and hang on to the handlebars to guide it. I was totally unaware that you needed to use brakes to stop it or slow down once in a while.

We lived on the main street of town not far from service stations and other businesses. I got on the bike right in front of our house. The street had a gentle slope toward town. Well, maybe it wasn't so gentle, anyway the bike started going a lot faster than I wanted to go and I didn't know what to do.

Ray must have realized I was headed for trouble but he didn't know what to do either.

He sounded angry when he started shouting, "Stop! Stop now! Mama doesn't want anyone riding my bike. Stop I said! Oh she's gonna kill me if you wreck my bike. Get off of it! Please."

You can never imagine how badly I wanted off. I saw the swinging sign in front of the service station looming ahead of me. I was headed straight for it faster and faster but I couldn't think to turn the handle bars. All I could think of was to hang on to them for dear life. It made a loud crashing sound when I ran the front end of the bike into the metal swinging part of the sign. A man in a green uniform with a star on it came running out of the station.

"What in the hell are you doing? I'm tired of you kids playing around here. Now get that bike and get out of here."

His swinging sign was swinging by only one chain and he was trying to hook the other side back on the frame. I could tell he was mad.

I wasn't going to bawl but Ray came and said, "She took my bike and my Mom's gonna be madder than a mad hornet when she sees my bike. I think the wheel is crooked."

I sat there on the hard cement driveway looking at my bleeding scraped knee and I couldn't keep from crying. My wrist hurt too and my elbow. I was going pretty fast when I hit the sign.

Ray picked up his bike and walked it home mumbling something about me. The man went back in the service station and I went home. Mama saw my knee the first thing.

"What happened to your knee?"

I hurried into my room. "Nothing happened. It was just an accident."

I must confess we did pester that man at the service station a lot and he had good reason to be angry with me that day. I don't know why we used his restroom all the time but it seemed we couldn't go past there without going in. Some kids lived a long ways away and it was more convenient. Sometimes, there were five or six of us, and when we finally came out there would be a line of tourists in a hurry to get in.

There were some little pink deodorizing things hanging on a nail on the wall. Why we ever decided to steal them, I have no idea. I can't think of more worthless things to steal. They smelled terrible. Steal sounds so criminal I think I'll say we took them. There was one in the Ladies' and one in the Men's so Jane had to get hers from the Men's. I already had mine dangling from my hand. She stood peeking out the door like a look out in the movies and when he had his back turned to gas up a car, we ran for home with our stolen goods.

Now I knew Mama thought stealing was an even worse sin than telling lies. The way my stolen goods stunk Mama would know something foul was going on the minute I walked in the house with it. So, I buried it by the front step before I went in and I guess the evidence of the metal container is still buried there to this day.

The next time we went to use the service station restroom the door was locked, and from then on everyone had to get a key to use it.

But after we asked for the key which he wouldn't give us and before we could get away from there the man in the station followed us out.

"Did you girls take the deodorizers out of the restrooms?"

"What's a deodorizer?"

He explained what they were. "They disappeared the last time you two were here."

We never went back again.

I never rode a bike again either until I was in my sixties and I bought my first bike which I rode hundreds of miles over deserts, mountains, seaside bike paths, roads and trails all over the western and southwestern states. Now I ride my mobility scooter in some of these same places.

Chapter 35

Nothing made me happier while we were living in Truckee than having Bill say, "Let's go for a ride."

There were so many places to go and things to see around Truckee. Bill kept an interesting conversation going all the time. He knew so many things to talk about and he included me in every adventure he took Mama on. It was Bill's nature to be kind and thoughtful of others. He couldn't have been any better to me and though Papa would always be first in my heart, Bill was also a good father to me.

There was one thing that plagued me almost every time we went for a ride. I always had to sit in the back seat and I think there must have been exhaust fumes in cars of that vintage. I would get so carsick sometimes that it would ruin the day for everyone. I heard lately that if you close one eye when you get motion sickness it stops. I wish I had known that then.

I remember one time in particular which almost makes me ill now just thinking about it.

Mama worried about me getting pimples like most teenagers did in those years. I never see young people with pimples now. I guess that problem has been solved. In those days you were told that almost everything gave you pimples but especially chocolate and me being a chocoholic Mama was concerned about me now approaching my teenage years.

"Ruthie, I want you to start eating one of these yeast cakes every day. I read in a magazine that eating yeast would keep you from getting pimples and you have to quit eating chocolate too. Chocolate is really bad for you. It makes your face break out with pimples."

I had seen other kids with faces full of pimples so I was willing to eat the yeast.

Along with so many other ideas about health they used to think chocolate was bad for you but now they think it is good for you so I still indulge in my addiction to chocolate.

I'll never forget that first yeast cake if I live to be a hundred. It was a hot day and we went for a ride to Nevada City to explore the mines where the 49er's found all that gold. The fumes in the back of the car were even worse in that hot weather. I felt dizzy. The yeast started boiling in my stomach. I felt it bubbling around. It began working like it was getting ready to make bread. It rose up into my throat. It tasted like yeast only worse than when it's still fresh. I doubled up with cramps in my stomach every time it churned extra hard.

"Stop the car! I'm very, very sick. I think I'm going to die. Oh, owie, my stomach. Stop the car!"

Mama could never have run fast enough to ever give me another cake of yeast and to this day I can't stand the smell of it. The carsickness bothered me to the point that I didn't want to go for car rides any more.

"Why don't you go and let me stay home? I can stay with one of my friends."

"No, you are going with us. We will stop if you get sick. You can sit in the middle in front and maybe that will help. I think it would help if you ate something but you never want to eat."

Bill had some time off and he was anxious to visit the dam being built in Nevada because it would be the largest dam in the world when it was finished and he had helped drill for the dam site. I couldn't convince them to let me stay home even when I told them I would just ruin their trip.

It's a long ways from Truckee to the southern tip of Nevada and I sat in the backseat most of the time as we traveled down through Nevada all the way. Now, I've heard other people describe that route and even in modern cars they don't enjoy it. For me a miracle took place on the long trip right there in that back seat of that old car.

It was hot. I gazed at the nothingness through my window and suddenly everything came alive for me. I kept searching for new things and I saw things that I had never seen before because the desert is the only place you find them. It is truly alive and some of nature's best paintings appeared unexpectedly before my eyes. There were small animals and unusual plants and trees even wild burros some places. The ocotillo and saguaro cactus and Palo Verde and Joshua Trees take their important place in nature. I discovered the desert is filled with beauty if you look for it and the splendor of it all is overwhelming.

The miracle I experienced there on the desert also took away my carsickness or else I never paid any attention to it any more.

"Oh look, look! There is a man on a lake in a row boat!"

"Sure enough, I see him too Ruthie."

Bill laughed at Mama and me.

"You two are seeing a mirage. Guess it's the first one you ever saw. It is common to see them on the desert."

He explained what caused mirages. I have been over that same route many times as an adult and there are no mirages. I've been told it has something to do with so much pollution in the air.

When we arrived at Boulder Dam, which they later changed to Hoover Dam, we were taken on a tour by Bill's boss. We got to go down inside where they were working pouring cement. It seems I remember seeing trains on tracks they used to move cement mix, tools and everything else. The dam site was really huge and a very busy place with lots of workers.

There has always been an ongoing rumor that men were buried alive accidently when they poured the cement for the dam and their bodies were never recovered but are still there in the dam. I learned this is just a myth and not true.

We visited Tent City where Bill's boss Mr. Gosset and his wife and daughter lived. He wasn't home very often because his job took him to many dam sites. Mrs. Gosset taught school there.

Of course, Tent City was called Tent City because it was a huge area full of tents and an amazing sight to see. The bottom half of the tent was built with boards and then covered with a pointed canvas top.

I'm trying to think what they did about toilet facilities. There must have been a community building for showers. I wouldn't even try to guess how many people lived there in those tents put up there for the workers on the dam but it looked to me like thousands.

I can't remember her name now but his daughter became my instant best friend. You know how it is. You meet someone new and instantly feel like you've known them forever. You just hit it off right from the first. We had something in common and that was our love for the outdoors and everything out there.

She had a pet Gila Monster she had caught and kept hanging in a bucket outside her tent door. You might wonder. "What is there to love about a Gila Monster?"

Well there are lots of things, for instance they are so ugly they are cute. They are colorful. And, how many pets could you get to live in a bucket hanging by the front door? I've heard they don't poop either. I don't know for sure how they dispose but I think I know.

They have only one really bad feature about them. Their venom is poisonous. You need to be aware of that if you decide to get one for a pet. The good thing I read recently is that this venom contains something that is proving to be very helpful in the treatment of type two diabetes. Everything in nature is good in some way and a benefit to mankind that's why we should take care of all of nature and not kill off anything or any part of it with our carelessness. Who knows, the lives we save in nature may someday save our own lives.

My friend took me out in the desert to find things to take home for souvenirs and then showed me all the beautiful things she had collected. I really liked the ribs from a saguaro cactus she had found some place else but Mama said there wasn't room for them in the car. Mama expressed a deep sigh of, oh no not again, when I loaded my collection of unusual and pretty rocks on the floor under my feet in the back seat.

We decided to visit Las Vegas while we were near there. I guess it was a gambling and entertainment city then. I don't remember that part about it. I know they had gambling in Idaho when I was young. It was sometime in the forties when they abolished gambling in Idaho.

All I remember about Las Vegas was going to see a movie. I'm pretty sure it wasn't a very big town and I'm positive it wasn't lit up as brightly as now because the electricity is brought in from the dam which wasn't completed at the time I was there.

The movie we saw was implanted in my brain forever. It was Top Hat with Fred Astaire and Ginger Rogers. That's when I firmly set my heart on taking dancing lessons before I went to Hollywood to become a movie star as I had been planning to do since early childhood. Oh, to dance like Ginger Rogers even if it was mostly backwards but with a leading man like Fred Astaire who cares if he gets most of the attention?

Chapter 36

One of the greatest opportunities of my lifetime came along and I wouldn't have missed it for anything no matter how carsick I might get riding in a car. Boulder Dam was finally finished.

"Pack your bags we are going to Boulder Dam. President Roosevelt will be there for the dedication ceremonies."

It was a thrilling time for me to get to see the President in person. I had seen other celebrity movie stars and I have seen and even met many other celebrities in my life but President Roosevelt stands out in my list as most important to me.

This was my second trip to the southwestern part of the United States. This time we traveled down through the middle of California instead of going through Nevada. I can describe it in one word. Colossal. I saw oranges on trees and date palms loaded with dates one of my favorite things to eat in the whole wide world. I saw fields of cotton and we stopped to swipe a ball of cotton, I had never even thought that my clothes were once growing on a bush until Bill told me my clothes were made with that very cotton growing in the field. I kept the ball of cotton for years.

On our way back home we stopped to see almost everything of interest. I have deep feelings of gratitude to think I was such a lucky child to see so many new things and have such lovely memories of them.

It was on this trip home that I experienced fear for my mother's life. Mama suffered her first heart problem as we were traveling through Indio in southern California. It turned out not to be serious but more of a warning and she recovered after one night enough to enjoy the rest of the trip. But, the worry about the future never went away. She had these incidents the rest of her life and they always scared me to death. I suppose as I think about it that it was angina but I didn't know in all those frightening years what it was.

President Roosevelt has always been my hero because of his wonderful plan of Social Security. Mama and I had been living on a shoestring and the shoestring often broke. It was a struggle for Mama to tie it back together and most of the time it didn't stay tied. Social Security for dependent children helped widows besides it was a perfect insurance plan for old age. I can remember people saying, "He is running up such a large national debt our children and grandchildren will have to pay for it. This is socialism."

I've heard this same woe is me phrase during some of the best times America ever had.

Some of the work done by WPA men and CCC boys is still being enjoyed today by those children and grandchildren. Perhaps they got their money's worth. I've always felt like we get more for our tax dollar than any dollar we spend.

I'm not sure about this but I think Bill must have rated a good spot near the President because he had worked drilling the dam site. We stood just a few feet from our President along with what seemed to be important people. His powerful voice rolled across the canyon and echoed from the hills. He was leaning on the podium. I never knew he was crippled from polio until years later. For some reason this was kept a secret during that time.

It wasn't long after that Bill's job took us to live in the southwest and my life was filled with new adventures and new sights the American Southwest has to offer. We have such an abundance to be grateful for in our beloved country.

Chapter 37

I turned around so I could see out the back window of the car. My eyes were misty and my vision blurred. I could barely make out the town through my tears but I had to have my last glimpse of Truckee, California and all I was leaving behind. The winter snow and ice skating on Donner Lake and the summer hiking and swimming in the Truckee River could never be replaced where we were going. I thought I would never be happy again. My heart sank even deeper as I wondered about the strange place where we were moving to in the southwestern town of Fort Sumner, New Mexico. There would be no snow in winter and only the hot dry desert in summer. Most of all I was concerned about going to a new school and meeting new kids.

The car was crowded with the four of us, Mama and Bill and Rex and me. It was a long trip in the 1930 sedan. It was hot. We had lots of flat tires and the radiator often spewed steam and water and we had to carry an extra water bag to replace it. There were a couple of cans of oil by our feet in the back seat. We stopped at filling stations for gas and water and oil. It was slow going in the car and took us about a week with all the stops we made to see the sights along the roadside. We stayed in tourist camps at night which were hard to find.

We drove into Fort Sumner and found the apartment that Bill's co-worker had already rented for us. Bill and Les had worked together for so long drilling dam sites they were very close so Les felt free to choose a place for us. This time it was a big surprise and we had to learn to like it. Our apartment was in the front half of a store that someone converted into two apartments. It was located exactly in the middle of town. Since Les got there first he took the back apartment.

Mama didn't know what to think about having a huge window right beside the sidewalk where people passed by constantly. There were thick lace ecru window curtains so Mama stood on the sidewalk and peeked through the window to see if she could see in our living room where we would be spending most of our time. She couldn't see us waving and grinning at her as long as the door to the kitchen wasn't open so a light shined through. We always kept the door to the kitchen closed so we could watch people and they couldn't watch us.

Sometimes things went on outside our window that were very interesting and almost as entertaining as going to a movie. There were people fights and dog fights and teenagers kissing on the way to school, mothers dragging bawling kids along after a spanking, cars broke down and being worked on, kids playing. It was a busy place. We got to know just about everything about everybody in town.

School was okay. The teacher remarked on what a good reader I was the first time it was my turn to read out loud. This made me work hard to keep her complimenting me on all my work. She had us sing songs and I wasn't good in singing but I learned the words fine. There was a very funny song about the states that I loved. The tune was so peppy it made me feel like dancing or marching like Mama and I used to do before Papa died.

Where did Ida hoe boys, where did Ida hoe? I'll ask you again as a personal friend, where did Ida hoe? She hoed in Maryland boys, she hoed in Maryland. I'll tell you again as a personal friend she hoed in Maryland.

There are many clever verses:

Where has Ore gone boys, where has Ore gone?

...He's seeing Okla home boys...

How did Wiscon sin boys, how did Wiscon sin?

...He stole the New brass key boys...

This delightful song about the states went on for several more verses. We loved it and sang to the top of our lungs. I still sing it.

There was only one thing that troubled me in my new school. A lot of the kids spoke Spanish and I felt left out because I couldn't understand them on the playground but I understood their English when they spoke English in the class room.

A very unusual thing happened during one of the winter months while we were in Fort Sumner. It snowed one day for the first time in over thirty years. The kids went wild and the principal dismissed school so they could go play in it. To me it seemed pitiful to watch them try to gather enough of that skimpy amount of snow to make snowballs and snowmen. I never heard such shouts of joy over snow in my whole life. I always had an abundance of snow in winters where I lived before.

Bill took us sightseeing around Fort Sumner so I got to see the grave of Billy the Kid. It was a hot dry place and a lot of snakegrass grew around there. It was called snakegrass because it crawled around like a snake and one had slithered across the grave of Billy the Kid. It was a very appropriate plant for that location because although you would think he was a hero the way they portray him he was really a scoundrel and doesn't deserve any bouquets. Souvenir hunters had chipped away a lot of the tombstone. I don't know what it is like around there now but as a child I thought the burial place was desolate and it made me sad.

A few miles away from the gravesite were the remains of the building where Sheriff Pat Garrett captured and shot Billy the Kid.

It wasn't far to Carlsbad Caverns from Fort Sumner. I didn't see as many of the caverns at that time as I saw in later years when I returned on an extended tour of New Mexico. By that time they had built stairs and elevators that led to much larger and many more caverns.

I consider Carlsbad Caverns to be the most spectacular display of nature's artwork in sculpture and color I have ever seen. It is beyond any words to describe it and must be seen to be appreciated. It certainly reminds you of how brief our time here on earth is when you realize the eons it took to make sculptures using drops of water. I can still feel the overwhelming sensation of watching nature's work of art in progress.

Our trip to the Petrified Forest in New Mexico was another unusual sight for me to see with Bill. We also visited some cave dwellings with nearby petroglyphs but I can't remember where they were. I tried to imagine what it was like to live in ancient times in a cave. All I visualized was a hairy man chasing after me with a big club. I wondered if kids went to school. I thought they must have for us to be so smart now. What a lucky child I was to see so many places and things to remember all my life. I loved moving so many times because there was always something new to see and learn about.

We weren't in Fort Sumner very long. In fact if I remember right I attended three different schools that year. Truckee, Fort Sumner and

Austin, Texas. The trip half way across Texas to Austin was another long hard trip. It seemed like such a long ways between towns to me. It made me feel cranky and my crankiness made the others feel cranky. I think. Anyway they didn't like anything I did like singing or fidgeting.

"Sit still. You're driving me nuts."

I didn't tell Rex I thought he was a little nutty too.

Service stations with small grocery stores and sometimes a bar were close enough together that we never ran out of gas and oil and water. I was bored and restless because I was a child. I hollered for a soda pop every time we stopped and anything else I thought I might get away with.

I remember the first time I heard the Texas drawl. The attendant at the service station dressed in cowboy boots and a cowboy hat sitting in the shade got up and moseyed over to the gas pump. He turned a crank and got the gas hose in his hand ready to gas up the car.

"Y'all want some gas?"

Rex was taking his turn driving the car. He couldn't keep from trying to be funny, "No thanks, just put some in the car please."

I'm not sure the attendant understood his sense of humor. A lot of his dry humor was never understood and I have the same problem with my sense of humor because I tried to copy everything my big brother did.

As usual, Les had already found a house for us. It was a very nice house with nice furniture and located on a lovely street. The trees and foliage around Austin were different and exceptionally beautiful. We had a majestic laurel tree beside our house with lovely white blooms. Some neighborhoods had black walnut trees which I didn't like to eat or gather because they tasted terrible and stained my hands. I can see the huge oak trees draped in Spanish moss around Austin and I'm thankful for the memory of everything I saw in my new surroundings.

A neighbor girl just my age lived across the street. I shyly wandered over to her yard to get acquainted. Her name was Wilby. We were soon chattering about school and other stuff. She talked funny like the man at the service station. I almost had to laugh when she asked me, "Y'all got a radio over at y'alls house?"

I almost used Rex's sense of humor and said, "No, not all of us. We just have one radio between us."

I caught myself just in time before I insulted her with my silly humor.

One of the first things I learned at the new school was that the kids thought I talked funny too and it wasn't long until I overheard someone call me the hillbilly from Idaho, but that was the least of my worries.

At that time, Austin was the seventh largest city in the United States. I never dreamed there was a school as big as the Junior High I got lost in on my first day of attendance. I never heard of Junior High before. The schools I had attended before were elementary and then High School. In this school, Junior High was the seventh, eighth and ninth grade and then there was High School. I always stayed in one room with one teacher in other schools but in this school I had to go to a different room and teacher for every class. There were several buildings and some of my classes were in another building. I wouldn't even try to guess how many students there were all together but I had never seen so many kids my age in my life. It was scary. I was continually late getting to my classes because I couldn't find the rooms or the building where I should be.

When I finally did find my room the classes I attended weren't even taught in the schools I had gone to before. For instance, my class in drafting where we sat at tall drafting tables on tall stools and had strange measuring instruments that we drew funny lines with. I was so baffled by that class I know I didn't learn a thing about drafting.

I had a hard time even sitting on the stool for such a long time. It always reminded me of a teacher that brought a tall stool to class and called it the dunce's stool. She told us how in the past they put a dunce's cap on kids and made them sit on the dunce's stool if they didn't learn their lessons. She never made anyone sit on the stool but she threatened to. Because I couldn't understand drafting I felt like a dunce sitting on that tall stool in drafting class.

We had typing class and the other kids were getting pretty fast at typing but I had started around the middle of the year and I was still doing the beginning exercises. I felt like a dunce in typing too.

Then there was algebra in the seventh grade. Math was never one of my strong subjects anyway and to be hit suddenly with algebra was another disappointment to my ego. I had always felt pleased with my report cards and now my grades were failing. It's good we didn't stay long in Austin or I would probably have flunked that year.

Home economics was another new experience for me but I didn't have any problems with it so I decided being a dunce even though I wouldn't be able to do anything very brilliant with my life I would be able to make someone a good wife. I learned a lot of useful things in that class that I have used all my life. We cooked some great meals, desserts and breads which we got to eat, but we had to eat our failures too.

The cafeteria was wonderful. I had never seen anything like it where you could choose whatever you wanted for lunch. I always packed a homemade lunch in other schools and I remember how I hated taking Mama's baked bread because all the other kids had store bought bread and tuna fish sandwiches instead of ham or peanut butter and jelly sandwiches on homemade bread like I had.

Everything cost a nickel apiece at the cafeteria and for a quarter we had great choices to pick a nice big lunch from. One item I chose everyday was corn bread that had been baked in a special iron that made it shaped like an ear of corn. It was swimming in brown gravy with small pieces of roast beef floating through it. I never had any trouble finding the dining room building. The wonderful aroma of good food led me right to it.

Chapter 38

I walked several blocks every Saturday to where I took a trolley to downtown Austin. That probably wouldn't be very safe for a twelve year old to do now. I liked to go to the five and ten cent store where I spent a lot of time looking at stuff and took my time deciding what I would choose to buy with my half dollar Bill gave me every week. I had already spent twenty cents for my round trip trolley ticket and I would need ten cents for the picture show.

There was the ice cream parlor where I got off the trolley to walk home and I always got a triple decker ice cream cone which was a nickel a scoop but the scoops were so big I could get by with one scoop if I found something I really wanted at the five and ten cent store.

The Beautiful Lady in Blue was a popular song at that time and they often played it while I was in the store. It just started playing in my head while I was typing this story. Now it will take the rest of the day to get it off my mind.

The beautiful lady in blue. She thought I was someone she knew. But her lips so divine were not meant for mine. Guess that's all I remember.

Sometimes I bought a pretty clip to wear in my hair or a shiny pin for Mama for a nickel before I went to the picture show.

Our country was very unkind to the black people at this time in our history. Segregation separated most of Austin. I can't remember I ever saw a black person before I moved to Austin and even then I didn't see very many. They stayed mostly in what was called their part of town and attended segregated schools. I'm sure there must have been quite a large community of African Americans but I seldom saw them. Racism is still a sad flaw our country endures but Texas at that time was much worse in my opinion than any place now.

Next door to where Les and his family lived was a family of midgets as they were called in those days. Now they would rather be called little people just as deaf people would rather be called deaf instead of deaf and dumb. Still, every once in a while due to ignorance you hear people referred to by these other terms.

Someone told me this little family was the only one in the world where every member was little. Usually at least one of the children will be the usual height. They had a car that had been adjusted to their size and since Les and his family became good friends with them they included me in their outings and we became good friends too. One thing I remember about the mother was that she was very strict and she didn't make any bones about correcting me if she thought I needed it. It seemed funny to me to be looking down at that little woman bawling me out and shaking her finger at me. I had a notion to pick her up and spank her.

There were two other outstanding events that are impressed in my mind from the time I lived in Austin, Texas.

Admiral Richard Byrd made his first scientific expedition to Antarctica in 1928. I met him on the steps of the capitol building in Austin in 1935. He had just returned from another trip to Little America the scientific base he established on his first expedition. He gave a long speech and I was standing close to him. Byrd had so much publicity and became so well-known during his life that Congress bestowed the title Rear Admiral Byrd on him. I've since met people that have never heard of him. I'm asking, "Do we still have history classes in school?"

There was always a huge crowd everywhere I went but the crowd that day seemed even larger and there were a lot of policemen around controlling it. I got groped by a policeman. It was the only time in my childhood anything like that ever happened to me nor had I even heard very much about sex. I think most children at that time were so innocent, at least the ones I spent time with. It seems to be different nowadays and children are no longer innocent but well informed by the time they reach the age when I was still so innocent.

The second and most outstanding event of my rather short time in Texas was an overnight train trip our class went on to visit the Alamo and then Galveston. Our class occupied one whole car on the train but even then not everyone got to go. Some of the kids' parents wouldn't let them go and some couldn't afford it is just my guess. It comes to me that we had to pay for everything we had at school because I remember riding the city bus to school and I had to pay for bus fare.

We had so much fun on the train that we stayed up most of the night. We played games, talked, raised heck and sang all the popular songs.

I have been to the Alamo in the last few years and I didn't remember it looking then like it does now. It seemed to me it didn't have so many nearby buildings but it must have because the walk we went on I noticed the dates on all the buildings were in the 1800's. I remember it sitting alone in a dry desert like place and now there is nice foliage around. I bought a plaster of paris model of the Alamo that could be used as a bank. I kept all my savings in it for many years.

I know we went on a tour of Galveston but the only thing I remember was the big ship in the bay and especially the sailors who showed us around the entire ship. Even though we were so young the sailors didn't seem much older and they flirted with us. I can still hear our shoes clanking on the metal steps as we toured every part of the ship.

Chapter 39

Soon after I returned from my great train adventure Bill announced they had finished drilling the dam site near Austin and we started packing to move back to California.

Kennett was the name of the little ghost town nestled in the Shasta Mountains where we would live while Bill worked at the site chosen for Shasta Dam. We chose our own new home this time because there were so many houses to choose from and besides we got there before Les so he didn't get to find a house for us.

There was still a train depot, post office, store, and of course the usual pool hall left in the ghost town but everything else had been abandoned and very few people lived there when we arrived. There were lots of nice houses and we chose one clinging to a hillside with the back of the house against the hill and the front half over the top of a small apartment.

Rex got the apartment at first but when he left to go back to Idaho I moved my things in it before anyone could say no. Imagine only twelve and I had my own apartment. Who could ask for anything more? Actually about all I did was sleep there. Mama wouldn't let me cook my own meals. It was nice to spend time reading there by myself unless I got lonesome, then I went upstairs. Kids liked to come and visit me after school and I could tell they envied me having my own apartment.

Kennett was a very important copper mining town until it was flooded by Shasta Lake while Shasta Dam was being constructed. Kennett is submerged under 400 feet of water and every time I go past there I try to figure out where I lived before it was flooded. It wasn't completely filled with water until 1944.

In the early days besides mining Kennett also grew as a result of railroad construction. There was a railroad camp established there for the workers and businessmen opened shops. The dam was started during the Depression in 1935 because of the New Deal government and most people were willing to sell their land to the government but a few stayed until the water came up to their property. They must have been the people that were still there when I lived there.

One room in our school held all eight grades of students. There was only one student in the 8th grade and the teacher spent a lot of time getting him ready for High School in Redding the next fall. She let older students teach the younger grades so she had more time for the 8th grader. It seemed strange because the older student didn't know as much as some of the younger ones did because they had heard the same things being taught in the same room to older students.

I finally got my ego back and decided I wasn't a dunce after all when the teacher told me I was very smart and put me up a grade.

Kennett was very pretty. The rocks in the surrounding canyon were red as was the dirt all around and it cast a rosy color on everything when the sun shined on it. It was quiet and peaceful after living in Austin. I still like being able to tell people I lived in a ghost town because I like to do things that are different and Kennett was about as different as any place you could ever live.

One day Mama kept me home from school which surprised me because she was a stickler for not letting me get away with pretending I was sick so I could stay home. She had a knack for getting to the truth.

"How sick are you? Let me see if you have a fever. Maybe you just need a dose of castor oil. Why don't you go to school and if you still feel sick at recess you can come home."

I got well as soon as she mentioned castor oil. You see Mama knew my tricks and she knew how to handle them. So why was she keeping me home from school? I thought maybe she was having one of her heart problems and needed me home. She kept to her room for several hours. I could hear her moving around above my apartment so she must not be too sick. When she came downstairs she looked tired and kind of sad.

Mama was sick all right with one of the worst kinds of sickness you can get. It had been bothering her for a long time. She was homesick for Idaho and her family and friends there. She had made plans to leave Bill but she couldn't face telling him. She knew he loved her and she thought a lot of him but it wasn't the same. Mama and Bill had planned to marry when we left Idaho with Bill, but she kept putting it off until now she knew she could never be happy moving so much and never having any friends. She kept hearing echoes from the hills in Idaho calling to her.

One of her boyfriends from Oregon from before she met Papa contacted her after Papa's death. He wrote letters to her even when she was with Bill and I guess she must have written to him too because he sent her the money to come home. He said he wasn't happy in his marriage and still loved her. He wanted to wait until his children were a little older before he got a divorce. I think men sometimes used that excuse for not getting a divorce and making changes that might mess up their comfortable life. Divorce was frowned on and could have affected his thriving business. I don't think he wanted a divorce. Anyway, he never got one. Mama waited and waited for him but I don't think I would have ever liked him.

I never knew this until I was much older and Mama told me all the details of that day when she came to my apartment and said to me, "Honey go put all your things you want to keep in the suitcase. You will have to leave behind anything that doesn't fit in it. Hurry we are leaving on the train in an hour to go back home to Idaho. I just finished packing our trunk and it is ready to go."

I went crazy with joy and jumped up and down. I could hardly wait to see my sister and brother and my niece and nephew. Idaho was still home to me even though my life was filled with so many new, exciting experiences.

Our neighbor stopped his pickup in front of our house and knocked on our door. When I opened the door he said, "Your mother asked me to take some luggage to the train. Is it ready to go?"

The neighbor left with the few belongings we were taking. About a half hour later, Mama and I started down the hill to the depot. I skipped ahead of Mama eager to get on the train.

About halfway to the depot we met Bill walking up the hill. I don't know why he happened to come home early that day. He must have realized by the look on Mama's face what she was going to say. He staggered as though his bad leg was about to give out from under him. I felt a sadness come over me even though I didn't understand exactly what was happening.

It hadn't dawned on me Mama was trying to get away without Bill knowing. She just didn't have the heart to tell him. I listened to their sad goodbyes, not realizing at first that I wouldn't be seeing the man who had been like a real father to me and who I loved. Suddenly I had mixed feelings about my future and the wonderful past few years we were with Bill. I thought about the years when Mama and I were so poor before Bill rode up in his big white car and rescued us. He always pampered us and I felt secure in his care. Where would we live? Would we go back to the hungry years before Bill? I felt torn between wanting to go back to Idaho and wanting to stay with Bill. Children adjust and accept but I didn't realize this. Still, I was excited to go back home in spite of my worry and sorrow.

Mama's voice almost failed her and she could hardly get the words out, "Bill, I'm leaving you. I have to go back home. I need my family and friends. I'm sorry."

It was one of the saddest moments of my life when he turned to me and said, "Write to me Ruthie and I'll send you a new coat every year."

That was the last I ever saw or heard of him. Mama didn't want me to write to him. She thought it best to let bygones be bygones.

The train brought us back to Idaho and we stayed a short time with my sister in Idaho Falls. I only had a few weeks left in that school year.

We were poor again, but my life was interesting during that time and I still hear echoes from Snake River Valley. It wasn't long until I had my thirteenth birthday and my life went through another big change. I will write about those teen years in my next book. I'm glad I met you and hope to meet you again. I hope you are glad you met me too. Have a nice day!

Update

My last trip to Ashton almost brought me tears. We stayed in the same log cabin motel that was there when I lived there. The woman that owned the motel told us we were lucky to get any place to stay because the town is usually booked full every night and only with reservations. They had a week or so of bad weather and several cancellations or we wouldn't have found anything in that area. The reason: People from everywhere including other countries have discovered what a great place Ashton is for recreation of every sort. There is hunting, fishing, hiking, winter sports and pristine sights to see. Ashton is close to other wonderful places like Jackson Hole and Yellowstone. It was not yet over-crowded when I was there about eight years ago.

The motel lady told us developers were arriving in droves from back east and other parts of the country. Down the road from her place I could see a big McDonald's and a hotel already built. My Doctor told me recently he went to purchase property in my hometown and the price of everything is so high he changed his mind about building a summer home there. If a Doctor thinks he can't afford the price that tells me it will only be for the very wealthy. I'm grateful I got to know how it used to be in the good old days.

You Can Go Back

They told me you can't go back and visit your past.
The places that you loved can never ever last.
They say there are changes all through the years.
And these changes will only bring you tears.
I started my journey with these warnings on my mind.
I was apprehensive about the changes I might find.
Can the clouds be as fluffy? Does the wind always blow?

Will the Tetons be as grand peeking through the snow?
Are there green rolling hills where our farm used to be?
Will the quaking aspen trees wave a welcome home to me?
Can I find all the turns on the washboard roads?
Maybe now they are paved to carry heavier loads.
My heart skipped a beat when I saw Ashton, Idaho.
We passed the same old school where I used to go.
Main Street looked the same as it did in the past.
I felt like a little girl that had come home at last.
I kept this child like emotion all along the way,
As we rode toward the farm it seemed like yesterday.
I was sitting beside Papa as the wagon bumped along.
Our horses Dick and Dan still looked big and strong.
There were green grain fields about three inches tall.
I imagined I could see the golden fields of fall.
Where is the prairie dog town? No sight of it around.
I suppose they dug up the farmer's newly planted ground.
That's where we rode old Jesse to get the mail each day.
There is a new road sign I wonder what it will say.
Hog Hollow Road. That's what the neighbors called it.
Because Papa raised hogs down the road from there a bit.
Our house burned down soon after we moved away.
But where the windmill used to be is there this very day.
I found a horseshoe that belonged to Dick or Dan.
It connects me to my past and you can go back again.

About the Author

Born in Idaho in the hills west of the Grand Teton Mountains, Ruth's sense of adventure was ignited at an early age and continued to motivate her as she worked as an airplane mechanic in WWII, raised a family in the Willamette Valley of Oregon and traveled America solo in her motorhome after retirement.

Ruth discovered her passion for writing during her golden years and hasn't stopped writing since! She finds inspiration in the beautiful people and places she has encountered in her life and her down to earth style gives her writing a charming appeal. Ruth is a member of several community writing groups and enjoys reading her poetry at open mics. *Echoes from the Hills of Idaho* is her first book of stories about her life. She is currently writing her next book, *Echoes from Snake River Valley.*

Made in the USA
Charleston, SC
31 March 2014